LABOR ON THE MARCH
THE STORY OF AMERICA'S UNIONS

BY THE EDITORS OF
AMERICAN HERITAGE
The Magazine of History

AUTHOR
JOSEPH L. GARDNER

CONSULTANT
BERNARD A. WEISBERGER
Adjunct Professor of History, New York University

PUBLISHED BY
AMERICAN HERITAGE PUBLISHING CO., INC.

BOOK TRADE AND INSTITUTIONAL DISTRIBUTION BY
HARPER & ROW

FIRST EDITION

© 1969 by American Heritage Publishing Co., Inc., 551 Fifth Avenue, New York, New York 10017.
All rights reserved under Berne and Pan-American Copyright Conventions. Library of Congress
Catalog Card Number: 74–88864. Standard Book Number: (trade edition) 8281–5015–X; (library edi-
tion) 8281–8013–X. Trademark AMERICAN HERITAGE JUNIOR LIBRARY registered United States Patent Office.

ARBITRATION IS THE TRUE BALANCE OF POWER.

Puck.— Don't meddle with the hands, gentlemen—this pendulum is the only thing to regulate that clock!

FOREWORD

There have been a good many foolish essays written upon the beauty and divinity of labor by those who have never known what it is really like to earn one's livelihood by the sweat of the brow. . . . Let such be silent.

Those caustic words were written by the poet John Greenleaf Whittier, who served for several months in 1844 as a newspaper editor in the thriving, allegedly idyllic cotton-manufacturing city of Lowell, Massachusetts. Whittier was one of the first to see the ugly reality of unregulated industrialization and to report it honestly. Factory hands at Lowell, many of whom were teenagers, were working twelve to fourteen hours a day, six days a week, for a weekly salary of $3.50 or less. And the few labor unions that existed in pre-Civil War America were too weak to make effective demands for better working conditions and higher wages.

The long struggle of America's workers to achieve equality and respectability goes back much further than Lowell in the 1840's, but it really is from that date that the story gains momentum. The highlights of the protracted and complicated contest between labor and management are presented in the text that follows. Other, longer volumes can be consulted for the complete history of the American labor movement, but the leading personalities and the most dramatic events of the chronicle are introduced here.

By the middle of the twentieth century, the American working man had won most of his demands for a better life: his hours of toil generally were limited to forty hours a week or less; his wages were subject to upward adjustment in line with the cost of living; and paid vacations, medical benefits, and retirement plans were standard features of most labor contracts. Yet unfortunately, just as the worker seemed to have achieved his goals, the unions became objects of widespread criticism. Revelations of the infiltration of Communists and criminal elements into American unions shocked and dismayed the country. But as the author of this book concludes, "the corruption of the few should not be allowed to obscure the accomplishments of the many; the Reds and racketeers should not overshadow the reformers." The story of America's unions is a dramatic one, with important lessons for all of the nation's citizens.

THE EDITORS

To prevent top-hatted Management from quarreling with Labor over workers' pay, Puck mounts the volume labeled Common Sense to replace the pendulum of Monopoly with Arbitration.

A number of AMERICAN HERITAGE
JUNIOR LIBRARY books are published each year.
Titles currently available are:

LABOR ON THE MARCH, THE STORY OF AMERICA'S UNIONS
THE BATTLE OF THE BULGE
THE BATTLE OF YORKTOWN
THE HISTORY OF THE ATOMIC BOMB
TO THE PACIFIC WITH LEWIS AND CLARK
THEODORE ROOSEVELT, THE STRENUOUS LIFE
GEORGE WASHINGTON AND THE MAKING OF A NATION
CAPTAINS OF INDUSTRY
CARRIER WAR IN THE PACIFIC
JAMESTOWN: FIRST ENGLISH COLONY
AMERICANS IN SPACE
ABRAHAM LINCOLN IN PEACE AND WAR
AIR WAR AGAINST HITLER'S GERMANY
IRONCLADS OF THE CIVIL WAR
THE ERIE CANAL
THE MANY WORLDS OF BENJAMIN FRANKLIN
COMMODORE PERRY IN JAPAN
THE BATTLE OF GETTYSBURG
ANDREW JACKSON, SOLDIER AND STATESMAN
ADVENTURES IN THE WILDERNESS
LEXINGTON, CONCORD AND BUNKER HILL
CLIPPER SHIPS AND CAPTAINS
D-DAY, THE INVASION OF EUROPE
WESTWARD ON THE OREGON TRAIL
THE FRENCH AND INDIAN WARS
GREAT DAYS OF THE CIRCUS
STEAMBOATS ON THE MISSISSIPPI
COWBOYS AND CATTLE COUNTRY
TEXAS AND THE WAR WITH MEXICO
THE PILGRIMS AND PLYMOUTH COLONY
THE CALIFORNIA GOLD RUSH
PIRATES OF THE SPANISH MAIN
TRAPPERS AND MOUNTAIN MEN
MEN OF SCIENCE AND INVENTION
NAVAL BATTLES AND HEROES
THOMAS JEFFERSON AND HIS WORLD
DISCOVERERS OF THE NEW WORLD
RAILROADS IN THE DAYS OF STEAM
INDIANS OF THE PLAINS
THE STORY OF YANKEE WHALING

American Heritage also publishes
HORIZON CARAVEL BOOKS, a similar series
on world history, culture, and the arts.
Titles currently available are:

CONSTANTINOPLE, CITY ON THE GOLDEN HORN
LORENZO DE' MEDICI AND THE RENAISSANCE
MASTER BUILDERS OF THE MIDDLE AGES
PIZARRO AND THE CONQUEST OF PERU
FERDINAND AND ISABELLA
CHARLEMAGNE
CHARLES DARWIN AND THE ORIGIN OF SPECIES
RUSSIA IN REVOLUTION
DESERT WAR IN NORTH AFRICA
THE BATTLE OF WATERLOO
THE HOLY LAND IN THE TIME OF JESUS
THE SPANISH ARMADA
BUILDING THE SUEZ CANAL
MOUNTAIN CONQUEST
PHARAOHS OF EGYPT
LEONARDO DA VINCI
THE FRENCH REVOLUTION
CORTES AND THE AZTEC CONQUEST
CAESAR
THE UNIVERSE OF GALILEO AND NEWTON
THE VIKINGS
MARCO POLO'S ADVENTURES IN CHINA
SHAKESPEARE'S ENGLAND
CAPTAIN COOK AND THE SOUTH PACIFIC
THE SEARCH FOR EARLY MAN
JOAN OF ARC
EXPLORATION OF AFRICA
NELSON AND THE AGE OF FIGHTING SAIL
ALEXANDER THE GREAT
RUSSIA UNDER THE CZARS
HEROES OF POLAR EXPLORATION
KNIGHTS OF THE CRUSADES

RIGHT: *In a detail from a 19th-century bank note two girls work efficiently in a cotton mill.*
NEW YORK PUBLIC LIBRARY

COVER: *Journeymen electricians march up New York's Fifth Avenue in a parade on Labor Day.*
WIDE WORLD

FRONT ENDSHEET: *A fabric of the 1870's shows scenes of a worker's home and factory life.*
METROPOLITAN MUSEUM OF ART, ROGERS FUND, 1948

TITLE PAGE: *Swarms of Chicago workers surround a speaker during the 1894 Pullman strike.*
STATE HISTORICAL SOCIETY OF WISCONSIN

BACK ENDSHEET: *New York's first Labor Day parade, in 1882, marches around Union Square.*
CULVER PICTURES

CONTENTS

	FOREWORD	7
1	VIOLENCE AT HOMESTEAD	10
2	COTTON GIRLS AND IRON MEN	24
3	THE KNIGHTS OF LABOR	44
4	SAM GOMPERS' QUEST	66
5	LABOR ON THE LEFT	88
6	A HOUSE DIVIDED	110
7	A TIME OF TROUBLES	126
	ACKNOWLEDGMENTS	148
	FURTHER READING	148
	INDEX	150

1

VIOLENCE AT HOMESTEAD

This idyllic view of Homestead was painted eight years before a brutal strike erupted.

The lookout stationed on Pittsburgh's Smithfield Street bridge peered down through the early morning fog at the murky waters of the Monongahela River. Lights downstream alerted him to approaching vessels, but he waited until the shadows took shape and passed under the bridge. Hurrying to a nearby telegraph office, the man sent a wire to the town of Homestead, a few miles upstream: "Watch the river. Steamer with barges left here."

It was not yet 4 A.M. on that morning, July 6, 1892, when Hugh O'Don-nell received the message from Pittsburgh. A leader of striking steelworkers at the Homestead plant of the Carnegie Steel Company, O'Donnell hastened to give the prearranged alarm for the expected arrival of the barges: a blast from the town's electric light plant whistle.

In a matter of minutes the town was in an uproar. Aroused from sleep, men, women, and children poured from their houses and milled through the town's steep streets and narrow, twisting alleys. A horseman galloped

A magazine artist showed another signal for the Pinkertons' approach: a flare alerting steelworkers on patrol at the river's edge.

through Homestead, crying out his confirmation of the news wired from Pittsburgh. The barges indeed were coming; on them were the hated and feared hirelings of the Pinkerton Detective Agency, presumably being sent to break the strike.

The confused throng of Homestead residents soon became a force with a goal and a mission. "To the river!" men began to shout. "The scabs are coming!" Those who were not armed with shotguns or pistols tore pickets from fences to use as clubs and joined the surge toward the riverfront steel plant. A fence at the company property line was easily pushed down and the mob gathered

on a hillside overlooking the boat landing. Daylight was breaking as the barges, drawn by the tug *Little Bill*, approached Homestead.

Inside the barges, the Pinkerton agents felt a sharp, sudden jolt as the tug pushed the vessels aground. Voices of an angry crowd reached the men, and warning shots fired from the shore alerted them to their danger. "Go back," someone was shouting. "Go back, or we'll not answer for your lives."

Some three hundred strong, the Pinkerton force had been recruited in the New York and Chicago areas for duty described as guarding a corporation's property. Two days earlier the recruits had arrived at Bellevue, Pennsylvania, several miles downstream from Pittsburgh, and had been put aboard the hundred-foot-long barges—one of which was outfitted as a dormitory, the other as a dining hall. Hull and decks of both were reinforced with metal plating. Some of the men remembered newspaper stories about the bitter strike at Homestead and made alarmed guesses that the Carnegie property there was the one that they would be guarding.

Now crates on the barges were pried open, and from them the officers of the force pulled Winchester rifles. They gave these weapons and fifty rounds of ammunition to each of the men who would take them. Some of the men—among them were drifters and college boys trying to earn extra money on summer vacation, as well as

In this detail from an 1892 pro-labor lithograph entitled "Great Battle of Homestead," strikers behind a barricade exchange fire with the Pinkerton agents aboard the two barges. At right, two men aid a stricken comrade, as another victim (center) is helped to the rear. Other casualties —dead or hurt—are shown.

professional detectives and experienced strikebreakers—refused the rifles. They had not been hired to fight.

A Pinkerton captain stepped out on the deck of the inshore barge. "We are coming up that hill anyway," he said to the sea of hostile faces, "and we don't want any more trouble from you men." Turning, he helped place a gangplank to the shore. "It's no use

A large piece of steel serves as a makeshift shelter for this Homestead worker, who keeps a careful eye on the detectives below.

returning the fire until some of us are hurt," the captain muttered.

Three strikers rushed to remove the gangplank, and one of them actually lay on it, daring the Pinkertons to step across his body. When the first agent down the plank stopped to shove the man aside, the striker pulled out a revolver and shot him in the thigh. Other bullets soon were whistling through the air; one Pinkerton fell dead, four others were wounded.

The agents on the barges promptly opened fire into the densely packed mass opposing them. Within three minutes thirty strikers had dropped; two of them had been killed instantly. Appalled, the two sides withdrew— the agents below decks on the barges, the strikers up the hill to seek shelter behind buildings or hastily erected barricades of scrap metal.

A number of the wounded Pinkertons were taken aboard the tug, and the *Little Bill* cut loose and drifted out into the current amidst another hail of

13

bullets. Inside the barges the men began to feel the morning sun beating down upon the roof above them. Firing ceased as the strikers on shore discussed their next move.

Hugh O'Donnell, a pale, slightly built young man of twenty-nine whose drooping mustache, bristling hair, and prominent ears gave him a somewhat fierce look, attempted to bring the situation under control. Although he was chairman of the strike-born union advisory committee, he had little control over the nonunion majority of Homestead's workers—many of them non-English-speaking recent immigrants. And his first offer to negotiate was rejected by the Pinkertons.

Through the morning the townspeople—now grown to an estimated ten thousand—continued to snipe at the Pinkertons every time one of the agents was brave enough to raise his head. Even a white flag hoisted on one of the barges was riddled with bullets. A few of the dispirited detectives

jumped in the water and attempted to swim to safety across the river; at least one of these was believed to have drowned. But most of the men huddled behind piled mattresses below.

Impatiently the strikers began devising other methods to flush out the agents. Dynamite sticks were lighted and tossed at the barges, but they bounced off with little effect. Oil was poured on the water upstream and set afire, but it burned poorly. When a cannon brought from a nearby town was trained on the barges, one of the balls killed a watching striker.

From Pittsburgh the county sheriff repeatedly wired Pennsylvania's governor for help in dispelling the armed mob, but the governor replied that local police must be used first.

By noon, eight strikers were dead or mortally wounded, and the mood on shore was violent. Union leaders attempted to reason with the workers, suggesting that the Pinkertons be allowed to leave. "Burn the boats, kill

In another detail of the 1892 lithograph, a detective boldly rushes ashore with a white flag of surrender. Although the fire from the workers' barricades seems momentarily suspended, a few agents can be seen huddling fearfully below deck.

the Pinkertons," cried the men. Not until five o'clock that evening did the union leaders get the mob to accept surrender of the detectives.

Running down to the barges, Hugh O'Donnell called to a Pinkerton captain: "This is enough of the killing. On what terms do you wish to capitulate?" The agents only wanted to escape, and O'Donnell granted them permission to come ashore and march to the railway station.

As the cowed detectives stepped ashore, they were quickly disarmed. A few were weeping as they lined up for the march through the hostile crowd. Behind them, townsfolk already were looting and burning the barges. Halfway up the hill the onlookers began punching the detectives and throwing stones at them. Women and children helped form a six-hundred-yard-long gantlet through which the agents were forced to run, warding off what blows they could. Before they reached the safety of a train, one hundred forty-three Pinkertons had been injured.

Nine strikers and seven Pinkertons died from the bloody day of violence at Homestead; another sixty on both sides were wounded by gunfire. And labor-management relations in the steel industry received a setback from which they were nearly a half-century recovering.

The Homestead steelworks covered six hundred acres along the Monongahela riverfront. With 3,800 workers

Harper's Weekly, JULY 16, 1892

Although armed workers tried to protect them as they marched to the train station, the Pinkertons were subjected to the taunts and blows of townsfolk lining the route.

on its payroll in 1892, it was one of the nation's major producers of iron and steel for buildings and bridges and of armor plate for the U.S. Navy. Valued at $6,000,000, the Homestead plant was only one of several Pittsburgh-area plants of the giant Carnegie Steel Company.

Andrew Carnegie's career was perhaps the most spectacular in American industry. In 1849 the thirteen-year-old son of Scottish immigrants had gone to work in a factory for $1.20 a week; a half-century later, he retired on a guaranteed monthly income of $1,000,000.

As early as 1889 Carnegie had relinquished operational control of his steel empire to Henry Clay Frick, another self-made man but one lacking Carnegie's unrivaled ability to get along with his employees.

In January, 1892, the Carnegie Steel Company called in officers of the Amalgamated Association of Iron and Steel Workers to discuss a new Homestead labor contract to replace the one that would expire the following June 30. The majority of workers in Pittsburgh's steel plants of that era put in a twelve-hour day, from 6 A.M. to 6 P.M. For backbreaking labor that also was generally hazardous, unskilled workers were paid as little as fourteen cents an hour.

Visitors always likened the steel plants to visions of hell. Men sweated in temperatures up to 128 degrees; a wrong turn could mean a scalding, a severed arm, or quick death. "You become more and more a machine," a worker complained to a visiting journalist; ". . . it drags you down mentally and morally just as it does physically."

Semiskilled workers of course earned more, and usually worked fewer hours, than did the common laborers. And the skilled elite among the workers sometimes got as much as $70 per week. Yet the average wage at Homestead was $100 per month.

To the workers' demands for stable wages and better working conditions Frick replied in January, 1892, with proposals that actually would reduce wages. Moreover, the company notified the men that future contracts would expire at the end of December

When these two photographs were taken about 1907, the lot of Pittsburgh steelworkers still was a miserable one. Above, two men team up to shape rods under a trip hammer.

rather than June. Even more than the reductions, the men feared the date change; if negotiations broke down in December, they would be forced to strike in midwinter when their families' needs for clothing and shelter were the greatest.

The Amalgamated Association, though one of the nation's strongest unions, represented only four hundred of the more skilled workers at Homestead; the remaining unskilled or semiskilled workers were nonunion men in whom the Amalgamated took little interest. Sensing a struggle ahead, the union launched a membership

16

As his two wistful children look on, a man who lost an arm in a mill accident poses for the camera—grim in the realization that he will not be compensated for his injury.

drive that added three hundred fifty more men to its rolls by June.

A self-styled philosopher, Andrew Carnegie once had written that the right of workers to form unions was "sacred." In May, 1892, however, Andrew Carnegie left on his annual pleasure jaunt to Scotland. On departing, he left Frick a memorandum to be distributed at his discretion: Homestead was to be made a nonunion plant. Frick pocketed the note and bided his time as fruitless negotiations with the Amalgamated dragged on.

In mid-June Homestead residents were surprised to see carpenters begin constructing a twelve-foot-high wooden fence surrounding the company property. When the walls were topped with barbed wire and searchlights were placed on platforms at frequent intervals, townspeople began joking—somewhat uneasily—about "Fort Frick." Portholes, three inches in diameter, were placed every twenty-five feet. Could they be firing positions, Frick later was asked? No, he replied, they were merely for peeking out to see who was passing by.

In secret, Frick wrote to the director of the Pinkerton National Detective Agency, an organization frequently used by management in its disputes with labor: "We will want 300 guards for service at our Homestead mills as a measure of precaution against interference with our plan to start the operation of the works again. . . ." He meant operation on a nonunion basis, for Carnegie had just cabled him from Scotland about the negotiations. "Perhaps if Homestead men understand that *non-acceptance means Non-Union forever*, they will accept."

On June 24 Frick gave the union twenty-four hours to accept the company's terms. When the deadline was reached, he announced that the wages were fixed. In Homestead it was payday, but little money was spent as men hoarded funds for the anticipated strike. The Amalgamated Association hastily formed a strike advisory committee, which was headed by Hugh O'Donnell.

Without warning, on June 28, Frick laid off eight hundred men in two Homestead departments; that night effigies of Frick were hung from a telegraph pole. It was clear to the Amalgamated Association that Frick would use the lockout—a deliberate shutdown of operations and exclusion of men from a plant—as a means to break the union. A mass meeting of union and nonunion men was called for the evening of June 29, at the Homestead Opera House.

"This is not a strike," one of the Amalgamated leaders shouted. "We filled our contract. Now the firm has laid the entire mill off one day ahead of time. Has it lived up to its contract?" "No, No, No," came the chorus of replies, as union and nonunion men alike voted to form a solid front against management.

By Saturday, July 2, the last employees had been laid off by the company. To Pittsburgh reporters the firm announced that Homestead would be

In later years Andrew Carnegie, shown scattering money in this 1903 cartoon from Judge, *was hailed for his charities. He endowed many public libraries across the United States.*

operated as a nonunion mill; there would be no further conferences with the Amalgamated Association.

The Fourth of July was one of the two holidays granted by the Carnegie Steel Company (the other was Christmas). This Fourth, 1892, was unusually quiet, however. All the furnaces were out at the mill, and hundreds of pickets surrounded the plant; men in a chartered paddle-wheel steamer and in smaller skiffs even patrolled the river. The Amalgamated's advisory committee virtually ruled the town; all discussions of the work issues were barred from saloons and other public places where arguments might erupt.

Rumors circulated that Pinkerton agents would be brought to the plant to protect strikebreakers. As the foggy night of July 5 approached, elaborate signals had been arranged to notify the town of the arrival, most likely by water, of the strikebreakers.

The "Battle of Homestead" on July 6 made shocking headline news across the nation the next day. From Scotland, Carnegie cabled Frick: "All anxiety gone since you stand firm. Never employ one of those rioters. Let grass grow over works . . ."

Three days later the Allegheny County sheriff wired the governor. "The situation at Homestead has not improved . . ." The strikers actually controlled the town, he complained. "Only a large military force will enable me to control matters. I believe if such a force is sent the disorderly ele-

Hugh O'Donnell posed for this picture some years after his strike ended in defeat.

ment will be overawed and order will be restored."

Reluctantly, the Pennsylvania governor called out a division of the National Guard and dispatched it to Homestead. Asked by a reporter if the troops were for the protection of nonunion men who wished to return to work, the commanding general, George R. Snowden, replied: "The gates are open and you may enter if the company permits it."

As the Pennsylvania troops went into bivouac on the hills overlooking the steel town, however, employees of six other Pittsburgh-area mills of the Carnegie Steel Company went out on sympathy strikes.

On Friday, July 15, three days after the arrival of the Guard, smoke started curling out of chimneys at the Homestead plant. Strikers rushed to the fence and tried to peer through

Frick (left) was the victim of an assassination attempt on July 23. Wishing to assist the Homestead workers, a young anarchist, Alexander Berkman (center), forced his way into Frick's office and shot him. Frick soon recovered, but Berkman and his accomplice, Emma Goldman (right), went to prison.

to see if the works were being started up again. The next day the company posted a notice giving workers until 6 P.M. Thursday, July 21, to report to work. Not one did so.

Inside the fence at the Homestead works, carpenters began building dormitories and dining halls for the strikebreakers who were being recruited throughout the eastern states. The tug *Little Bill* and another steamer began a shuttle service, bringing workers— mostly illiterate and unskilled recent immigrants from Eastern Europe—to the boat landing.

Modest strike benefits were paid to both union and nonunion men at Homestead but soon the Amalgamated had to call for financial assistance from other unions across the nation. Many families were evicted from company-owned houses and strangers from out of town took their place.

On August 4 it was announced that soldiers would escort strikebreakers to work at the nearby Duquesne plant, one of the six Carnegie works on sympathy strike. Fearful of losing their jobs permanently, the nonunion men stampeded back to work and the strike was off there by August 8. At another plant the Amalgamated accepted the company's offer to reopen and union men marched back to work in a body. At the end of the month Frick visited Homestead itself and announced that the strike was over. Some of the troops were recalled, and picket lines were reduced to a token force at the plant's main entrance.

Fights continued to break out between individual strikers and the scabs, and on October 6 explosives were tossed in the window of a hotel operated for strikebreakers. Nevertheless, a week later, the last soldier was pulled out of Homestead, and law enforcement was left to local agencies.

On October 15 the Homestead newspaper sadly announced, "The Great Homestead Strike is gradually dying out." Two thousand workers, including two hundred former strikers, were now at work in the plant, the paper reported.

Carnegie, privately backing Frick to the hilt, expressed public agony over the strike to British Prime Minister William Gladstone: "This is the trial of my life," he said hypocritically. "It is expecting too much of poor men to stand by and see their work taken by others. . . . The pain I suffer increases daily. The works are not worth one drop of human blood. I wish they had sunk."

At a meeting of strikers on Saturday evening, November 19, fiery speeches calling for continued resistance were delivered. Significantly, however, a vote was postponed until the following morning. Only some three hundred workers showed up for the final strike meeting, and not all of those raised their hands when the vote was taken, 101 to 91, to declare the mills open.

On Monday morning, November 21, some five hundred strikers appeared at the company gate to apply for work. The new plant superintendent, Charles M. Schwab, spent until 4 P.M. that day reviewing the applications, but many of the strikers had been blacklisted and now were forbidden re-employment.

There already were 2,715 men working at Homestead on the day the strike officially ended. Two weeks later only 406 of the 2,200 strikers who applied had been hired. The others gradually packed up and left town to find work elsewhere. Hugh O'Donnell, denied re-employment, became the manager of a touring vaudeville company.

During the Homestead strike an estimated $850,000 was lost in wages; the state bill for calling out the militia was fixed at $440,246.31. Carnegie Steel never reported its expenses for attempting to reopen the works during the strike, but the firm's profits at the end of the year were $4 million, down only $300,000 from the previous year.

Low wages and long hours continued at Homestead and most other steel plants for at least the next twenty years, or until the increased production caused by the outbreak of World War I in 1914 led to greater prosperity throughout the nation. In 1907 a reporter found the average unskilled laborer at Homestead earning $16\frac{1}{2}$ cents an hour, only $2\frac{1}{2}$ cents more than in 1892. "A man works, comes home, eats and goes to bed, gets up, eats and goes to work," one said of his life.

Following its defeat at Homestead the Amalgamated Association of Iron and Steel Workers went into a slow decline from which it never recovered. Attempts to re-establish union lodges at Homestead failed when company spies reported secret organizing meetings. "If you want to talk in Homestead, you must talk to yourself," became the rule for steelworkers there.

Encouraged by Carnegie's triumph over the union, other steel companies resisted workers' organizations as well. By 1909, the Amalgamated Association was in effect banned from all plants of the U.S. Steel Corporation, successor to Carnegie's firm. Not until 1937 did the firm recognize a union.

Writing his autobiography a few years later, Andrew Carnegie—who had abandoned industry for philanthropy—wrote sadly: "No pangs remain of any wound received in my business career save that of Homestead. It was so unnecessary. The men were outrageously wrong."

The violence at Homestead in 1892 was one of the most dramatic confrontations between labor and management in United States history, but unfortunately, the tragic events enacted there were not unique. Intense rivalry and bitter hatred—leading in this case to bloodshed and death—characterized much of labor's long struggle for recognition and equality. With the defeat at Homestead, that struggle seemed lost. Yet curiously, only a half-century earlier America had seemed to some observers to be a workers' paradise.

Under a shower of sparks from a Bessemer converter, steelworkers strain to pour the molten metal into ingot molds. This view of a Pennsylvania steel plant was painted in 1895.

Tending the machines that produced cotton thread was not an unpleasant occupation, according to this 1825 lithograph, one of a series that showed various stages of cotton manufacturing.

2

COTTON GIRLS AND IRON MEN

The visitor from England was duly impressed by the famous cotton mills of Lowell, Massachusetts.

"I happened to arrive at the first factory just as the dinner hour was over," he wrote, "and the girls were returning to their work; indeed the stairs of the mill were thronged with them as I ascended. They were all well dressed . . . They were healthy in appearance, many of them remarkably so, and had the manners and deportment of young women: not of degraded brutes of burden."

The year was 1842, and the celebrated English novelist Charles Dickens was paying his first visit to the United States. Among the leading American sights of the day—to which Dickens and other tourists from abroad invariably were directed—was the large and efficient cotton manufacturing center at Lowell, a town located on the Merrimack River some twenty-five miles northwest of Boston.

Lowell's modern factories, and the apparently happy girls who worked within them, never failed to excite the wonder and admiration of these visitors. Passing from praise of the comely factory hands to a description of the plants, Dickens continued:

"The rooms in which they worked, were as well ordered as themselves. In the windows of some, there were green plants, which were trained to shade the glass; in all, there was as much fresh air, cleanliness, and comfort, as the nature of the occupation would possibly admit of . . ."

The mills at Lowell were only two decades old at the time of the novelist's visit. The Industrial Revolution that already had transformed Dickens' England from an agricultural economy to one based on manufacturing was beginning to affect the United States as well.

Prior to the American Revolution the colonies had imported most of their manufactured goods from the mother country. In the years after it won its independence, the young nation struggled to build industries that could fill its own citizens' needs. The creation of a cotton manufacturing system is one example of America's early movement toward industrialization, and the factories at Lowell were that industry's showcases.

During the years 1810–12 an enterprising Bostonian named Francis Cabot Lowell traveled through England, studying that country's cotton manufacturing. But England's laws forbade the export of machinery; it did not want to share its leadership in the Industrial Revolution with other countries. Therefore, when he returned home, Lowell had to smuggle sketches for industrial machinery out of the country.

In 1813 Lowell and a group of business associates formed the Boston Manufacturing Company and purchased a site for cotton mills at nearby Waltham. He personally supervised the construction of machines to spin thread and weave cloth.

At first there was some resistance on the part of buyers to cloth made in America, but soon the Waltham mills were turning out "thirty miles of cloth per day." Lowell died in 1817, at the age of forty-two, but his partners decided to carry on and even expand the industry he had created.

Outgrowing the Waltham site, the Boston cotton manufacturers began looking for a location that would offer a large tract of uninhabited land and—more importantly—abundant water to keep the machines running. The place they picked was a farm area along the Merrimack River, where a series of rapids builds up the needed water power. A canal on which their products could be transported conveniently linked the site to Boston. On February 6, 1822, the Merrimack Manufacturing Company was incorporated, and two months later the associates began laying out a town, appropriately named Lowell.

Three five-story mills were built parallel to the river, the one at center topped by a white cupola. Three additional plants were placed at right angles to them, and the area in between was landscaped with trees and shrubs. The place could have been mistaken for a college campus.

At Waltham, Francis Cabot Lowell had staffed his cotton mills mainly with New England farm girls, reasoning that they already would have learned weaving and spinning at home. Factory employment offered them a way of earning some money while they waited for marriage proposals. At Lowell this system was extended, and soon employment agents in long black wagons were combing the countryside to find eligible girls.

To house these girls at Lowell, semidetached frame dwellings were built; the cost of board and room in these houses was deducted from the girls' weekly salaries. Male employees were put up in less comfortable brick dormitories.

By January, 1824, the Lowell mills were turning out printed calico cloth. And at the end of its first decade as a factory town Lowell had expanded to nineteen plants. Of its 12,000 inhabitants, 5,000 were mill workers; 3,800 of these were the already famous Lowell girls. That year, 1833, President Andrew Jackson paid

America's first cotton mill was built in 1790 at Pawtucket, Rhode Island, by Samuel Slater, who—two decades before Francis Lowell—memorized plans for its machinery in England.

a visit to Lowell and on a pleasant day in June reviewed a parade of the mill workers. Dressed in white muslin, all wearing blue sashes and carrying green parasols, 2,500 of the girls marched past two abreast. "Very pretty women, by the Eternal!" the aging general was heard to mutter as he bowed to the girls.

Word of Lowell's busy factories and its supposedly happy workers soon reached Europe, where the evils of industrialization—crowded cities; noisy, dirty, and unhealthy factories; long and often hazardous labor at machines for low pay—already were apparent.

A visiting Englishwoman named Harriet Martineau marveled at tales of how the Lowell girls not only supported themselves comfortably on their wages at the cotton mills—two or three dollars per week above board and room—but also were able to put money in the bank. Some indeed were said to have earned enough to pay off

27

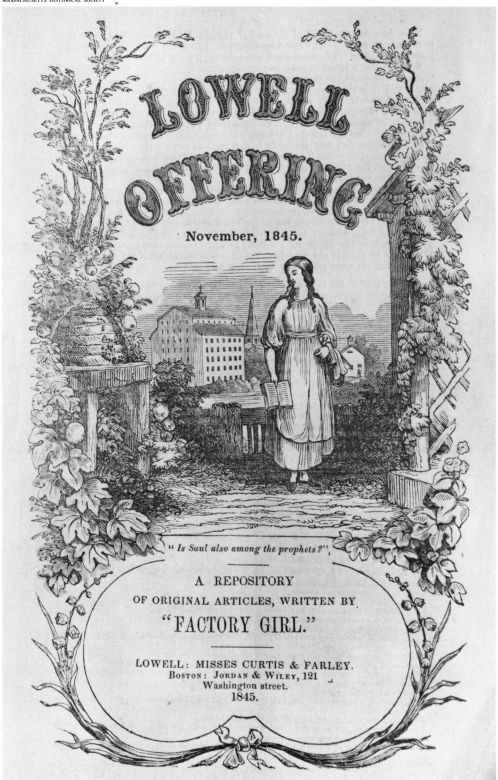

LOWELL OFFERING

November, 1845.

" Is Saul also among the prophets?"

A REPOSITORY
OF ORIGINAL ARTICLES, WRITTEN BY
"FACTORY GIRL."

LOWELL: MISSES CURTIS & FARLEY.
BOSTON: JORDAN & WILEY, 121
Washington street.
1845.

The title page of the Lowell Offering *gives a romanticized picture of a working girl—book in hand in a leafy arbor. In actuality, factory work left very little free time for reading.*

the mortgage on a father's farm or send a younger brother to college.

"I saw a whole street of houses built with the earnings of the girls," Miss Martineau wrote, "some with piazzas and green venetian blinds; and all neat and sufficiently spacious."

One of the town's unique institutions was *The Lowell Offering*, a newspaper written and published by the mill workers in the 1840's. The stories that the Lowell girls wrote for their newspaper often were only autobiography disguised as fiction. And the pictures they gave of life in Lowell was considerably less attractive than the accounts of Charles Dickens and other visitors.

In one story a character lamented: "Up before day, at the clang of the bell—and out of the house by the clang of the bell—into the mill, and at work, in obedience to that ding-dong of a bell—just as though we were so many living machines."

At one time the factories opened at 7 A.M. But overseers complained that the girls were "languorous" if they ate before arriving, and the work day was advanced to 5 A.M.—with time out for breakfast at seven. This meal, like the dinner at 12:30 P.M., had to be downed in thirty minutes—including the time it took to walk, or run, from the factory to the boarding house and back.

The length of the working day varied from season to season, and quitting time was stretched to 7:30 P.M. during longer summer days. It made

for a working day of up to thirteen and one-half hours. For a six-day week of eighty-one hours, a Lowell girl received a salary of $2.50 to $3.50. From this sum $1.25 or more was deducted for board and room. There were generally only three or four holidays per year. If a girl wished to take a few weeks off for a summer vacation, usually to return home to help on the farm, she did so without pay.

Harriet Martineau gave a rosy picture of a young girl's arrival at a cotton mill:

When a girl comes to the overseer to inform him of her intention of working at the mill, he welcomes her and asks how long she means to stay. It may be six months, or a year, or five years, or for life. She declares what she considers herself fit for, and sets to work accordingly. If she finds that she cannot work so as to keep up with the companion appointed to her, or to please her employer or herself, she comes to the overseer and volunteers to . . . pick cotton [from the floor], or sweep the rooms, or undertake some other service that she can perform.

A character in another story written by a Lowell girl for *The Offering* gave a rather different impression of a worker's first day:

At first the sight of so many bands, and wheels, and springs in constant motion was very frightful. She felt afraid to touch the loom, and she was almost sure she could never learn to weave. . . . It seemed as if the girls all stared at her, and the overseers watched every motion, and the day appeared as long as a month had at home. . . . At last it was night. . . . There was a dull pain in her head, and a sharp

pain in her ankles; every bone was aching, and there was in her ears a strange noise, as of crickets, frogs, and jews-harps all mingling together.

To launch their enterprise and to attract farm people to an entirely new and different way of life, the owners of the Lowell mills had set up a basically benevolent and attractive factory system in the 1820's. But the 1840's were not the 1820's, and by the time of Charles Dickens' visit, the Lowell girls were beginning to feel oppressed by the tyranny of long hours and low salaries.

During the nineteenth century the United States experienced a series of financial panics, or depressions, that always seemed to affect the people at the bottom of the economic ladder most seriously. The panic of 1837 was one of the most severe such shocks to America's economy, and its effects were felt throughout the next decade.

Waltham's cotton sheeting, which had sold for thirty cents a yard when it first was produced in 1816, was commanding only six and one-half cents a yard in 1845. To offset these falling prices, New England mill owners increased the work load and cut the wages of their employees. In a period when many corporations failed to pay dividends or went out of business altogether, the Merrimack Manufacturing Company of Lowell continued to make a healthy profit.

In 1842 highly skilled weavers— the best-paid workers at Lowell— were receiving $3.84 per week; three years later, they were getting $3.48. Wages for less skilled workers fell from $3.40 per week to $2.76. Since the amount deducted by the company

In 1833 Lowell—depicted in the color lithograph at left—was a charming town of neat red-brick buildings in a handsomely landscaped setting along the Merrimack River. Another idyllic view of factory life is presented in Winslow Homer's painting Morning Bell (below). Carrying lunch pails, girls saunter across a bridge toward a local factory.

for board and room remained the same or even rose, this meant an actual drop in earning power of from 14 to 30 per cent.

Lowell itself was becoming a less attractive place to work. In the 1840's the semidetached houses separated by gardens or lawns were torn down and replaced with rows of tenements on narrow alleys. A visitor found one house in the center of town with 120 residents; a single room held a family of ten and four adult boarders.

To keep profits high, the owners began paying overseers bonuses for increased production; the foreman achieved the increased output—and his bonus—by exploiting the girls.

For the lesser pay they were receiving in the 1840's the girls were expected to do more work. In the 1820's each girl had been assigned to two looms. Now they were being forced to tend three and even four looms, all operating at increased speed. Those workers who refused found themselves out of work—and unable to find employment elsewhere because their names had been placed on a company blacklist.

Against such oppression by their employers the operatives of New England's cotton mills had little protection. The tradition of workers banding together in unions was an old one in the United States but it was not really a very strong one.

As early as 1778, New York printers had gone on strike to demand a mini-

THE TRIAL

T. Wharton

OF THE

Journeymen

BOOT & SHOEMAKERS

OF PHILADELPHIA,

ON AN INDICTMENT

FOR A COMBINATION AND CONSPIRACY

TO RAISE THEIR WAGES.

TAKEN IN SHORT-HAND,
BY THOMAS LLOYD.

PHILADELPHIA:

PRINTED BY B. GRAVES, NO. 40, NORTH FOURTH-STREET,
FOR T. LLOYD, AND B. GRAVES.

1806.

The minutes of a historic trial of 1806, in which Philadelphia shoemakers were convicted of conspiracy merely for organizing to raise their wages, was printed as a pamphlet.

mum wage. Shoemakers in Philadelphia established the nation's first continuous organization of wage-earners fourteen years later; after a two-year interval, they reorganized themselves as the Federal Society of Journeyman Cordwainers—a group that lasted to 1806.

In succeeding years printers, carpenters, shoemakers, tailors, cabinetmakers, coopers, and masons in other cities—New York, Boston, Pittsburgh, Washington, Baltimore, New Orleans —formed similar associations. They tried to protect their position as skilled workers by limiting the number of unskilled apprentices admitted to their trades and by attempting to maintain adequate prices for their products. Although these early groups occasionally won their demands, they were not organized well enough to last any length of time.

American society was not quite willing to accept the principle of collective bargaining, whereby union members present their demands in a group and refuse to settle for anything less as individuals. And some early court decisions even held that unions on strike were illegal conspiracies.

In addition, it proved difficult to make workers themselves believe in unions. The boom and bust of America's unregulated free economy contributed to the impermanence of labor organizations. During depressions men were willing to work for almost anything; when good times returned, the workers too often saw no need for a union—they already were getting what they wanted.

Up to 1820 most American workers continued to be self-employed, often working right at home. Outside the cities at least, shoemakers, carpenters, and tailors worked at their trades only seasonally—usually during the winter months. At other times they were farmers or fishermen; the products of their trade merely brought in extra money for added necessities or even for an occasional luxury.

The introduction of the factory system at Lowell and elsewhere through-out New England and the Atlantic seaboard states changed the American work pattern forever. The skilled artisan working at home was replaced by the unskilled laborer working in a factory for an owner who often was either unknown or absent.

As early as 1828 several hundred women cotton mill operatives at Dover, New Hampshire, "rioted" because of oppressive working conditions. But these young ladies got nowhere. The terms of employment they —and other cotton mill workers in New England—signed were ironclad: "We, the subscribers . . . agree to work for such wages per week, and prices by the Job, as the Company may see fit to pay. . . ."

At the end of February, 1834, a 15 per cent wage cut had been announced at Lowell. Some 800 to 2,000 of the girls joined a "turnout" or strike, issuing a broadside proclaiming "Union Is Power." After two days of parading and speechmaking—and Sunday to

Before laws put a stop to the practice, small children were employed to perform difficult and hazardous jobs in many factories.

cool off—the operatives went back to work at the reduced wages.

Two years later, in October, 1836, the company announced that it was increasing the cost of board and room deducted from wages from $1.25 to $1.37½ per week; it was the equivalent of a five per cent wage cut.

An eleven-year-old girl, Harriet Hanson, took the initiative in one spinning room. "I don't care what you do," she announced to the other girls. "*I* am going to turn out, whether anyone else does or not." Most of the other workers followed Harriet out of the mill.

That day, 1,200 to 1,500 Lowell factory girls marched through the town's streets, singing:

Oh, isn't it a pity, such a pretty girl as I
Should be sent to the factory to pine away
    and die?

As their fathers had fought against British oppression in the Revolution, the girls were exhorted, so should they now resist the oppression of the factory owners. A Factory Girls Association of 2,500 was founded, but by the end of the month the girls were forced to return without the restoration of the wage cut.

In the following decade a more serious effort was made to unionize the Lowell girls. Five young ladies banded together in December, 1844, to form the Lowell Female Labor Reform Association. Dedicated to winning the ten-hour workday, but thoroughly expecting initial defeat, the girls took as their motto "Try Again." Within a year there were 600 members with branches of the association throughout New England.

Unions and reform groups had been petitioning Congress for legislation to limit the workday to ten hours since 1825. Yet not until 1840 did President Van Buren issue an executive order setting ten hours as the maximum workday for all federal employees.

In 1847 New Hampshire became the first state in the Union to pass a ten-hour law. Pennsylvania followed suit the next year, and during the 1850's Connecticut, Maine, Rhode Island, Ohio, Georgia, and California also limited the workday to ten hours.

Yet there was a big hitch to most of these laws: the ten-hour workday could be enforced only where there were no "special contracts" between employer and employee. Most factory owners got around the law simply by making the signing of contracts providing for a longer day a requirement of employment. A New Hampshire newspaper editor smugly commented on a situation unchanged by his state's new law:

The whole matter [of hours] is one which can best be regulated by those whom it most concerns—the employer and the employee. And such, we are happy to learn, has been the course pursued. The largest portion of those who are employed in our mills—working as they do by the job and piece—are desirous of working as many hours as they can. Those who take a different view of the matter seek other employers or different occupations. It is a free country.

One of labor's early friends was Horace Greeley, the eccentric, crusading editor of the *New-York Daily Tribune*. Outraged by the "special contracts" that circumvented ten-hour laws, he thundered in the columns of his influential newspaper:

To talk of the Freedom of Labor, the policy of leaving it to make its own bargains, etc., when the fact is that a man who has a family to support and a house hired for the year is told, "If you will work thirteen hours per day, or as many as we think fit, you can stay; if not you can have your walking papers; and well you know no one else hereabout will hire you"—is it not most egregious flummery?

While other states were at least making some effort to regulate hours of employment, Massachusetts—the home of the "model" factory system —procrastinated. Not until 1874 did Massachusetts limit the labor of women and children to ten hours per day. Long before the tardy action of the Bay State legislators, however, the halcyon days of New England's cotton mills had vanished forever.

By midcentury, New England's rocky soil no longer could yield enough farm produce to feed a rapidly growing nation, and many Yankee farmers were pulling up stakes and heading for the Midwest's fertile, wide-open spaces. The lure of California gold after 1849 took some

Easterners even farther west. And suddenly the farmers' daughters who once had made up most of the New England cotton mills' working force also were gone.

Meanwhile, because of the devastating potato famines in their native land, thousands of Irish immigrants were pouring into America's eastern seaports. The newcomers rapidly filled the jobs left vacant by departing workers of native Yankee stock, and soon one half of Lowell's operatives were Irish.

It was a cruel irony that made many humble tillers of the soil in the Old World factory workers in the New. "Remember the American cities are not the homes you seek for," one Irish immigrant wrote a cousin in the old country. "Get out of them as fast as you can either on foot or otherwise. Face toward the setting sun."

Unfortunately, few immigrants from Ireland, or from other European countries, could heed this sound advice. Most of these newcomers never got much farther than the eastern seaboard cities. Swelling America's population enormously, they also were creating a new urban, industrial class in the United States.

The optimism of the 1820's had given way to the despair of the 1840's and the 1850's. "There is at this very moment," the editor of a workingman's newspaper wrote in 1845, "a great strife between capital and labor and capital is fast gaining the mastery. . . ."

In 1849 Dr. Josiah Curtis made a pioneering study of the effect of factory employment on health and reported to the American Medical Association in grim terms: "There is not a state's prison or house of correction in New England where the hours of labor are so long, the hours for meals so short, and the ventilation so much neglected as in the cotton mills with which I am acquainted."

News of a May, 1851, strike by Philadelphia carpenters to raise their wages twenty-five cents per day—to $10.50 per week—set Horace Greeley to pondering. Carpenters, he knew, already were among the best-paid workers in the land. How could a man support himself, a wife, and say, three children on anything less than that sum? To establish this point, Greeley drew up a sample budget.

In commenting on his list of expenditures, Greeley asked his readers: ". . . have I made the working-man's comforts too high? Where is the money to pay for amusements, for ice-creams, his puddings, his trips on Sunday up or down the river in order to get some fresh air, to pay the doctor or apothecary, to pay for pew rent in the church, to purchase books, musical instruments?" It was a rhetorical question, one that needed no answer. There was no money for luxuries in the average workingman's wages.

During this same period a visitor to Fall River, Massachusetts, interviewing the overseer of a cotton mill, asked if the company ever did any-

thing for the physical, intellectual, or moral welfare of workers.

"We never do," he replied. "As for myself, I regard my work people just as I regard my machinery. What they do or how they fare outside my walls I don't know. . . . When my machines get old and useless, I reject them, and get new, and these people are part of my machinery."

New-York Daily Tribune, MAY 27, 1851

Labor Movements in Philadelphia.
PHILADELPHIA, Friday, May 16.
To the Editor of The N. Y. Tribune:

I again lay hold of the pen to chronicle the transactions of the Workingmen of this city during the last two or three weeks. The Eight Hour question continues to be debated with unabated vigor and enthusiasm. This reform is certain to take place, whether immediately or remotely no man can possibly say. The Carpenters of our city are upon a strike for an advance of 25 cents a day; this will make $10 50 a week. I propose to examine this matter and see if $10 50 be too much for a workingman at the week's end. We will reason fairly on this subject. Take a workingman at from 30 to 40 years of age, with his wife and three children I wish to be not in extremes, for although in some families the number of mouths to be fed are fewer than five, yet in other families there are six, seven, and even ten or twelve persons; but to take away all opportunities of dissatisfaction I will average the family at five.— Now what will it take to maintain a family of the last mentioned number weekly—"aye, there is the rub." We must now analyze, we must now cast accounts; no mock pride, no maudlin sentimentalism shall deter me from dissecting this matter in all its parts, and probing this social ulcer to the very quick. This article will be read and treasured up by workingmen in all sections of the country.

A barrel of flour, $5, will last 8 weeks—this will leave flour 62½ cents per week, sugar, 4 lbs at 8 cents per lb, 32 cents per week, butter, 2 lbs at 31½ cents per lb, 62½ cents, milk, 2 cents per day, 14 cents per week; butcher's meat, 2 lbs of beef at 10 cents per lb per day, $1 40 cents per week, potatoes, half a bushel, 50 cents, coffee and tea per week, 25 cents; candle-light, 14 cents per week; fuel, 3 tuns coal, $15, per annum; charcoal, chips, matches, et cetera, $5 year. This makes 40 cents per week for fuel. Salt, pepper, vinegar, starch, soap, soda yeast, now and then some cheese, eggs, &c. 40 cents a week more, for all these sundries; wear and tear and breakage of household articles, such as cups, saucers, plates, dishes, pans, knives, forks, &c. &c. 25 cents per week; rent $3 00 per week; bed clothes and bedding 20 cents; wearing apparel $2 00 per week; newspapers 12 cents. Let us now sum all up:

Flour	62½	Sundries	40
Sugar	32	Household articles	23
Butter	62½	Bedding	20
Milk	14	Rent	3 00
Butcher's meat	1 40	Wearing apparel	2 00
Potatoes	50	Newspapers	12
Tea and Coffee	25		
Candles and Oil	14	Total	$10 37
Fuel	40		

The sample budget printed in Greeley's New York Tribune *revealed that necessities would take $10.37 of a $10.50 weekly wage.*

The 1830's had seen the establishment of several workingmen's parties, in which laborers sought to better their condition through direct political action—such as the agitation for ten-hour-day laws. Through the next decade associations of workers embarked on other crusades—for free education, currency reform, and co-operative societies in which the workers would own the factories. Most of these activities were short-lived and unsuccessful. This was not to be the direction in which America's laboring force would move.

Modern American trade unionism, as it exists even today, emerged in the 1850's.

Attempting to maintain or raise their standard of living, skilled workers increasingly sought to distinguish themselves from the masses of common laborers, especially immigrants. The organizations they formed to promote their own interests in this period incorporated most of the ideas that have dominated the labor movement ever since—although many of these policies were not fully developed until two or three decades later.

Among the union policies initiated or first given strong endorsement by workers in the 1850's were rules for apprenticeship; the closed shop, in which only union members were allowed to work; insistence upon uniform time and method of payment; initiation fees and dues for union membership; funds for strike benefits; union employment offices or hiring halls; salaried union officers; union lobbies in Washington to promote labor legislation; and exclusion of all nonworkers from union membership.

Perhaps the most important development of this period, however, was the establishment of national trade unions, starting with that of the printers in 1852. Other national organizations—leagues of existing local unions—were launched to represent upholsterers, hat makers, plumbers, railroad engineers, stonecutters, lithographers, cigarmakers, carpenters, painters, cordwainers, and machinists and blacksmiths.

Although the ideas of modern unionism developed slowly and individually in all these different trades, a picture of the emerging labor movement in America can be formed by a review of one national union—the iron molders—and its forceful leader, William H. Sylvis.

America's most notable early union chief was born in western Pennsylvania on November 28, 1828. The son of a journeyman wagonmaker, William Sylvis had to make his own way in life, and at the age of eighteen he became a helper in the local ironworks.

An apprentice iron molder in those days made about $2 to $4 per week, but at the end of his apprenticeship he was rewarded with a "freedom suit"—an outfit consisting of a broadcloth suit, white shirt, woolen hose, calfskin boots, and a tall silk hat. As such a qualified craftsman,

Sylvis found work as an iron molder in a Philadelphia stove foundry.

By midcentury, the United States was embarked on a course of industrial growth that would make it the world's leading manufacturing power, and the iron industry was one of the most rapidly expanding sectors of the economy. The lot of the ironworkers, however, aroused the pity of the *Atlantic Monthly*, which described them as: ". . . masses of men, with dull besotted faces, bent to the ground . . . begrimed with smoke and ashes, stooping all night over boiling cauldrons of metal . . . breathing . . . an air saturated with fog and grease and soot, foulness for soul and body . . . their lives were incessant labor, sleep-ing in kennel-like rooms, eating rank pork and molasses, drinking—God and distillers only know what. . . ."

A union of Philadelphia iron molders was founded in 1855, but it was not until two years later—in December, 1857—that Sylvis joined the group. A 12 per cent wage cut had been announced for his factory, and Sylvis was among those who walked out on strike. Within a month the twenty-nine-year-old ironworker was corresponding secretary of the union; the rest of his life was to be dedicated to union causes.

Some years later Sylvis was to write that ". . . those who are forced to prominence in the labor movement sleep on no bed of roses." In addition

An 1856 lithograph depicts an iron foundry at Paterson, New Jersey, as a frantically busy place, with men sweating and straining to produce steamboat and railroad equipment for America's transportation industry.

to expected attack from management, he asserted, labor leaders "receive a fire in their rear from those who ought to be their friends . . . they are assailed with fault finding, their motives are impugned, and sometimes even private as well as public character is assailed."

Union officers in those days generally were paid no salaries, and union business was attended to only in the evenings, after a man had put in ten or more hours at the factory. His long hours of work for the union, Sylvis

once joked, made him a traitor to the eight-hour-day movement.

As secretary of the Philadelphia union, Sylvis soon was corresponding with iron molders' groups in other cities, and on December 14, 1858, he issued a call, in behalf of his own organization, for a national convention of ironworkers.

Responding to Sylvis' summons, thirty-five delegates representing the iron molders of thirteen cities assembled in Philadelphia on July 4, 1859. Unfortunately, the delegates at this historic first convention could decide on nothing more noteworthy than to call another meeting—early the next year in Albany. At the 1860 meeting Sylvis was elected treasurer.

Later that year, however, the new treasurer was charged with embezzlement of union funds, and the Philadelphia local refused to send him as a delegate to the third national convention, in Cincinnati, in January, 1861. Incensed, Sylvis paid his own way to Ohio, successfully refuted the charged of mishandling union funds, and was awarded $100 for his expenses during the preceding year.

During 1860 a number of iron molders' stikes had been called across the country—and some even were successful. But 1861 proved to be a bad year for the union. Striking iron molders at Troy, for instance, were rehired only after they signed a statement promising to withdraw from the union.

This was the year of Abraham Lincoln's first inauguration, secession, and Fort Sumter, and interest in union activities dwindled in the rising crisis of civil war.

"It having been resolved to enlist with Uncle Sam for the war," one group of workingmen declared as the firing began, "this union stands adjourned until either the Union is safe or we are whipped."

Thrown out of work by a temporary economic slump, Sylvis and a friend raised a company of volunteers to fight for the North, but his military career was short-lived. When he could not get near the fighting, he resigned in disgust.

Workingmen, Sylvis had noticed, were not participating fully in wartime prosperity. Prices ran ahead of wages in a rising spiral. The well-to-do could purchase exemptions from the draft for $300, but others—including the national president of the iron molders—fled to Canada to evade military service. Troops actually were called out to break strikes.

The weakened iron molders union held no convention in 1862. When news reached him that the national treasurer had been killed in battle, Sylvis took matters in his own hands.

Backed by the Philadelphia local, he called for a convention to be held in Pittsburgh in January, 1863. At that meeting, twenty-one delegates from fifteen locals unanimously elected William Sylvis national president.

During several trips that year—through the Midwest to St. Louis; north to Ottawa, Canada; east through New England; a total distance of 10,000 miles—William Sylvis almost literally built with his own hands the Iron Molders International Union. (In the names of American unions, *International* denotes United States–Canadian membership.) Starting out with only a $100 gift from his Philadelphia local, Sylvis begged rides in engineers' cabs when he did not have train fare and boarded with union members en route. Later his brother pictured him during these trips:

He wore clothes until they became quite threadbare and he could wear them no longer. . . . The shawl he wore to the day of his death . . . was filled with little holes burned there by the splashing of molten

William Sylvis

iron from the ladles of molders in strange cities, whom he was beseeching to organize.

At the 1864 convention, held in Buffalo, Sylvis could report triumphantly that thirty-six locals had been founded or reorganized and that national membership had risen from 2,000 to 3,500. "From a mere pigmy, our union has become a giant," he proudly announced to the delegates. The grateful convention re-elected him president and—in an unprecedented step—voted him $350 for expenses during the past year, and a salary of $600 for the coming year.

The 1865 iron molders' convention in Chicago was called the "largest Convention of Workingmen of one craft ever held on this continent," but under Sylvis' tireless prodding the union grew even larger and stronger in the next two years. By 1867, the Iron Molders had reached a membership of some 9,000. This was 75 to 85 per cent of all journeymen within the areas over which the union claimed jurisdiction.

During these years Sylvis was successful in establishing many precedents that would serve the union cause well in the decades to come. In addition to holding annual conventions and paying salaries to national officers, the Iron Molders under his leadership collected dues (50 cents a month by 1867) from members and were thus in a position to distribute funds to strikers.

The national organization also authorized legal strikes and curbed wildcat or illegal ones. A union press was encouraged, and members were disciplined with outspoken notices in these papers: "The following parties have sold out their carcasses:" and "Keep your eye on a small piece of humanity that worked here for two weeks . . ." Scabs who worked in defiance of an authorized strike found it next to impossible to find work anyplace where the Iron Molders' union had jurisdiction.

Sylvis also was among those championing the eight-hour day in the post-Civil War period. By 1868, a number of state legislatures, including New York, Wisconsin, Illinois, Missouri, Connecticut, and California, actually had passed eight-hour laws. The Iron Molders' chief was a member of a union delegation that pressed the eight-hour day on President Andrew Johnson, and in June, 1868, Congress

41

made eight hours the legal workday for all federal employees.

Sylvis already was turning his attention to wider interests. Nearing forty, a man of medium build, he seemed to possess inexhaustible stores of energy. He had a ruddy complexion, a light beard and mustache, and bright, intelligent eyes.

In February, 1866, Sylvis had met with the presidents of the coachmakers' and printers' national unions to draw up an agenda for a convention that would embrace all the trades. Illness prevented him from attending the Baltimore conclave that established the National Labor Union in August, 1866, but at the third meeting of this budding national organization, in September, 1868, William Sylvis was elected president. Under his leadership the NLU tried to fuse such diverse elements as trade unionists, eight-hour-day agitators, farmers, women's rights advocates, and emancipated Negroes. Sylvis was hopeful that out of it would grow a national labor party capable of electing the next president of the United States in 1872. There even was talk of Sylvis as a vice-presidential candidate on one of the major party tickets.

"I love this Union cause," Sylvis once told a labor convention. "I hold it more dear than I do my family or my life. I am willing to devote to it all that I am or have or hope for in this world."

During early 1869 Sylvis made an extensive swing through the South to organize in behalf of the Iron Molders and the National Labor Union. He was in Philadelphia that summer preparing for the August convention of the NLU, when he suddenly complained of severe stomach and bowel pains. Early on the morning of July 27, 1869, William Sylvis died, a few months short of his forty-first birthday.

"Sylvis! The National Calamity" ran the headline of one union newspaper; another printed its front page with a black border. Around the nation, unions passed laudatory resolutions, and from Europe came a letter of sympathy signed by, among others, Karl Marx, the founder of international Communism.

Sylvis left a widow and five sons virtually penniless; to finance the NLU convention that summer, he even had mortgaged the family's furniture. The costs of Sylvis' funeral were borne by the iron molders of Philadelphia.

The NLU convention was held as scheduled the month after Sylvis' death, but the group tried to pursue too many reform goals. Without Sylvis' dynamic leadership, the organization, at the end of three years, vanished from the American labor scene.

Yet within five months of William Sylvis' untimely death, and in his home town of Philadelphia, another group of workers was to establish the nation's first truly powerful national labor organization.

Reaffirming Andrew Johnson's endorsement of the 8-hour day for federal workers, President Grant issued this proclamation in 1869. He guaranteed the same wages for fewer hours of work.

LEADERS OF THE KNIGHTS OF LABOR

3

THE KNIGHTS OF LABOR

The meeting of the Philadelphia garment cutters' union was called that evening, December 9, 1869, to consider the group's steady decline. After little or no discussion, a resolution was offered and adopted by a nearly unanimous vote: "To dissolve and divide the funds among the members in good standing."

During the Civil War the tailors of Philadelphia and other Northern cities had been kept busy sewing uniforms for the huge armies raised to put down the Southern rebellion. In 1862 the Philadelphia garment cutters had organized a union to keep non-qualified workers out of their trade.

Younger men coming into the business after the war did not appreciate the union's role in establishing their prosperity, and membership in the garment cutters' association sagged. During the summer of 1869 one of the union's founders, Uriah S. Stephens, began pondering the

Terence Powderly, the erratic Master Workman of the Knights of Labor, dominates this 1886 poster. At the top is Uriah Stephens, founder of the Order and its first leader.

group's future. Stephens once had considered becoming a minister, but the panic of 1837 had forced him to abandon his studies and take up the tailor's trade in Philadelphia. Something in his religious background, apparently, made Stephens think of a workers' organization that would bind men together in a mystical brotherhood.

After the resolution to dissolve the garment cutters' union was passed on December 9, Stephens and eight other tailors adjourned to a nearby hall. One man was selected to stand guard at the door as the others excitedly made plans for a new, secret society. Within three weeks the nine tailors had held two more meetings, and on December 28 they adopted a name for their fledgling body: the Noble and Holy Order of the Knights of Labor. Two days later, at a fourth secret gathering, six additional members were admitted.

On January 6, 1870, the fifteen Knights of Labor elected their first officers. Stephens was made president with the title of Master Workman. The vice-president was to be called

Worthy Foreman; another officer was known as Worthy Inspector; and the Unknown Knight was to be in charge of applications for admission.

Like boys meeting in the family garage to form a neighborhood club, the Philadelphia tailors adopted a constitution and an elaborate ritual for their meetings.

Upon entering an anteroom, each Knight would take a card from a triangular table and write on it his name, as an indication of his literacy—in the Order's view a prerequisite to advancement. A knock on the inner door would draw the attention of the Lance, who would admit Knights to the sanctuary. In this inner sanctum every officer had a prescribed place to sit and symbols to denote his rank.

At each meeting two questions were put to the assembly: Were there any vacancies to fill in the trade? Were any brothers of the Order out of work or seeking new employment?

It was not the intention of Stephens and his associates to limit participation in the Order to tailors; in fact, the Knights of Labor from the beginning was envisioned as something much bigger and grander than any of the trade unions that had preceded it. The problem that the Knight-tailors confronted, of course, was one of spreading the word about a society whose members were sworn to secrecy.

In August, 1870, the handful of Knights voted to allow members to

OPENING SERVICE.

A Globe being placed on the outside of the Outer Veil; a copy of the Sacred Scriptures closed, and a box or basket, containing blank cards on a triangular Altar, red in color, in the centre of the vestibule; a Lance on the outside of the Inner Veil, or entrance to the Sanctuary, over the wicket; that the initiated may know that an Assembly of the * * * * * * * * are in session.

The M. W. will proceed to open an Assembly in due form as follows:

Precisely at the hour for opening, the M. W. standing at the Capital, shall give one rap and say, "All persons not entitled to sit with us will please retire." After a short pause, he will say:

M. W. The proper Officer will satisfy himself that all present are entitled to sit with us, and make the proper record.

The W. Ins. examines all present, and makes the proper record in the M. W. roll book. Members at a distance of three miles, or out of the State; any one reported sick, or Brothers absent from the city reporting by letter, receive a present mark. When done, reports as follows:

W. I. M. W., I have examined all, and will make the proper record.

M. W. W. F. see that the Veils are properly marked and securely closed. Allow none to enter or retire during the Opening Service, and that the O. Esq. and all Brothers are in the Sanctuary.

The W. F, after attending carefully to the duties reports thus:

W. F. M. W. the Veils are properly marked and securely closed, the O. Esq and all Brothers are in the Sanctuary.

Give three raps. The Organist may perform a symphony, and appropriate Odes may be sung, if there be such arrangements for music. The officers each bearing his standard and insignia of office, form a circle around the centre, at which is a square Altar, on which is spread open a copy of the Sacred Scriptures; the officers in position as near on a line from the centre to their stations in the Sanctuary as may be: the members, as many as can, standing by the side of the officers to form a complete circle or circles on the outside. Perfect quiet being had, the M. W. shall say an extract from the Sacred Scriptures appropriate to the occasion, such as this, for example:

M. W. Behold how good and how pleasant it is for brethren to dwell together in unity. It is like precious ointment upon the head, as the dew of Hermon, and as the dew that descended upon the mountains of Zion, for there the Lord commanded the blessing, even life forevermore.

Turning to the V. S. the M. W. shall say:

M. W. V. S. what are the duties of the M. W?

V. S. To preside with impartiality: see that all mandates are faithfully executed. In cases of emergency, where no law exists, to use his best judgment for the in-

*The ritual for meetings of the Knights of Labor (designated by ***** in the page shown) was as detailed and solemn as some religious services. It included organ music and Bible reading.*

tell other interested workmen that a secret society existed, although they still could not mention who belonged or breathe a word about the sacred ritual. Two months later, the first member of another trade was admitted to the society of tailors. After he and a few others of his trade were admitted, and had mastered the ritual of the Knights, they were allowed to "swarm" and form their own assembly.

Growth in these early years was slow, but by 1874 some eighty locals had been established in the Philadelphia area. Weavers, ship riggers, stonemasons, bag makers, machinists and blacksmiths, stonecutters, and wool sorters—all had their separate assemblies.

Early in 1874 locals were formed in New York; Trenton and Camden, New Jersey; and Boston. With the Knights of Labor well on the way to becoming a nationwide body, it became necessary to establish control over these far-flung groups. On December 25, 1873, the Philadelphia locals had formed District Assembly 1, and nearly a year later, District Assembly 2 was established at Camden.

By this time, the panic of 1873 had led to the most severe and what was to be the longest economic depression of the nineteenth century. As always before, unions collapsed during hard times when men were willing to accept any work at any pay. The miners of western Pennsylvania, left without their trade unions, began turning to

Inscribed on the emblem of the Knights was its hope for a government in which the injury of one would be the concern of all.

the Knights of Labor, and soon Pittsburgh became an even more important center of activity for the Order than was Philadelphia.

The men of Pittsburgh's District Assembly 3, formed on August 8, 1875, were not slow to challenge Philadelphia for leadership. Rival conventions were held at Philadelphia in July, 1876, and at Pittsburgh in May, 1877, but neither succeeded in establishing a national headquarters.

Continuing hard times led to widespread outbreaks of violence in the United States during the summer of 1877. Strikes of railroad workers against wage reductions turned into riots in Baltimore, Pittsburgh, and a dozen other cities across the nation, and in many cases federal troops had to be called out to restore order. Defeated trainmen also began looking to the Knights of Labor for protection from economic oppression.

As a compromise between the Philadelphia and Pittsburgh rivals, the first General Assembly of the

47

Harper's Weekly, AUGUST 11, 1877

Knights of Labor was convened at Reading, Pennsylvania, on January 1, 1878. Representing the Scranton District Assembly was a young railway machinist named Terence V. Powderly.

The eleventh of an Irish immigrant couple's twelve children, Powderly was born on January 22, 1849, at Carbondale, Pennsylvania. For a few years he attended the proverbial Little Red School House, but to contribute to the family income, he went to work as a switch tender in the local railway yards at the age of thirteen. At seventeen he became an apprentice machinist, and three years later he went to work in the Scranton shops of the Delaware, Lackawanna, and Western Railroad.

Early in his career as a workingman Powderly joined a union, a local of the International Union of Ma-

The illustrated press of 1877 printed such sensational pictures as these of the violent labor upheavals of that year. Railway strikes in Maryland, West Virginia, and Pennsylvania turned into bloody riots, and the disturbances soon spread across the country. At left, a mob draws back to watch Pittsburgh's Union Depot go up in flames. A determined lady (below) waves a pistol to signal her intention to keep trains running.

chinists and Blacksmiths. Then, in 1876, he began having serious discussions of labor problems with a fellow workman, and the two soon found that they shared many common beliefs. One summer evening the man asked Powderly to come along to a "labor lecture," but the two were kept waiting in a vestibule outside the "lecture hall." Years later, Powderly recalled what happened next: "Soon after a man wearing a black gown and mask came out to question us. He appeared to be more satisfied with our answers than I was with his appearance, for I had no thought of joining a society of any kind that night."

Nevertheless, Powderly, with no advance warning, was initiated into the Knights of Labor that evening, September 6, 1876. Upon his entry into the hall, all the members rose and

49

formed a circle into which the innocent candidate was ceremoniously conducted. After taking the oath, Powderly was informed that he was a member of the Order; only then did his friend reveal himself as the Unknown Knight.

Powderly was one of thirty-three delegates—from Pennsylvania, West Virginia, Ohio, Indiana, and New York—at the 1878 Reading General Assembly that succeeded in making the Knights of Labor a national organization. Membership was thrown open to all wage-earners and to former workingmen. Bankers, doctors, lawyers, and liquor sellers were excluded, and to this group of undesirables later were added professional gamblers and stockbrokers.

In addition to drafting and adopting a constitution, the Reading General Assembly dealt with the problem of secrecy. A faction at the convention fought to make the group's name public, as a first step toward full disclosure of their activities. They were outvoted, however, and for three more years members, in all their communications, had to refer to the organization as the Noble and Holy Order of *****.

Stephens was elected the first Grand Master Workman. The burdens of union office proved too much for him, however, and in 1879 Terence V. Powderly was designated as his successor. The new Grand Master Workman was just four months short of his thirty-first birthday.

For fourteen years, from 1879 to 1893, Powderly headed the Knights of Labor. He saw the Order balloon into the nation's largest labor group and then almost as quickly collapse.

During these crucial years, however, the Grand Master Workman as often as not was engaged in other activities. He served three two-year terms as mayor of Scranton and later was a county health officer. He was active in a group called the Irish National Land League and in the third party Greenback-Labor movement. He also found time to run a coffee and tea business with a brother-in-law and later was part owner and manager of a grocery store.

Furthermore, a good deal of the time that Powderly spent on union activities seemed to be taken with writing long letters to other unionists complaining that he did not have enough time. "I am literally deluged with letters. . . . I am pestered with invitations to attend banquets, entertainments, etc. I am besieged from every quarter to lecture. . . . I will not go. My throat is not strong enough to speak in public. . . . the Order has grown and is growing stronger every day, but I am not growing stronger and must have relief from unnecessary labor."

A slender man of less than average height, Powderly never was very hardy. He disliked the frequent travels that the Order's business necessitated and he suffered from recurring colds and other respiratory ailments.

A blond mustache drooped down over his mouth, and long, slightly wavy hair reached to his collar. Soberly dressed in black, with a stand-up collar and plain tie, he presented a most respectable appearance, according to a contemporary's description:

"English novelists take men of Powderly's look for their poets, gondola scullers, philosophers and heroes crossed in love but no one ever drew such a man as the leader of a million of the horny-fisted sons of toil."

Along with Powderly, many Catholics began joining the Knights of Labor, yet the Catholic Church was historically opposed to secret societies with vows and rituals that might come into conflict with the confessional.

In the 1870's a secret society of Irish-Americans known as the Molly

Maguires had terrorized Pennsylvania's mining districts with arson and murder. Allan Pinkerton's detective agency infiltrated the group, and with the arrest, conviction, and execution of several Mollies, the organization was destroyed. Nevertheless, many fearful citizens were to see in the rise of the Knights of Labor a resurrection of the Molly Maguires. Perhaps for this reason, the Catholic Church began denouncing the Order as early as 1878.

Even before he took over leadership of the Order, Powderly began pressing for an end to the secrecy that was hindering growth in addition to causing conflict with the Church. Not until the 1881 General Assembly, however, was a resolution passed to drop the words "Noble and Holy"

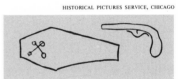

Crude drawings of a coffin and a gun were unmistakable messages delivered to intended victims of the Molly Maguires, a secret society of Irish-American laborers that flourished in northeastern Pennsylvania's anthracite coal areas in the 1870's. On the evidence of a Pinkerton agent who infiltrated the group, twenty-four Mollies were tried for murdering mine officials and ten were executed. At left is an artist's rendering of a nocturnal raid by a group of Molly Maguires.

51

from the organization's name, abandon *****, and at last let the world know that the group was called the Order of the Knights of Labor.

It was a small victory for Powderly, and he spent a few more years fighting for further revision of the ritual that would make it more acceptable to Catholics. In 1886 Powderly succeeded in convincing Cardinal Gibbons of Baltimore that there was nothing in the Order's constitution and practices that would be in conflict with a Catholic's obligations to his Church. On a trip to Rome the following year Cardinal Gibbons was instrumental in getting the Holy See to lift its ban on membership.

The question of secrecy was, of course, only a side issue with Powderly and the Knights. The group's true goal was to organize all working people in the United States so that, thus united, they could demand a greater share of the nation's prosperity. The demands inevitably led to conflict with management—and to strikes.

Strikes, however, were something Powderly could not abide. Toward the end of his career as a labor leader, he described his feelings:

All of this time I have opposed strikes and boycotts. I have contended that the wage question was of secondary consideration; I have contended that the short-hour question was not the end but merely the means to an end; I have endeavored to direct the eyes of our members to the principal parts of the preamble of our Order—government ownership of land, of railroads or regulation of railroads, telegraphs and money—but all of this time I have been fighting for a raise in wages, a reduction in the hours of labor. . . . Just think of it! Opposing strikes and always striking; battling for short hours for others, obliged to work long hours myself, lacking time to devote to anything else.

Ironically, in view of Powderly's vehement opposition to strikes, it was a series of strikes that was to bring the Knights of Labor to its peak of power —and sadly, to lead to its ultimate decline. The curious chain of events started in Denver, Colorado.

An itinerant printer named Joseph R. Buchanan helped establish a Knights of Labor local assembly in the Mile High City in November, 1882; the following month he brought out the first issue of *The Denver Labor Enquirer*. Soon Colorado workers began looking to Buchanan for leadership.

To save time and money, Buchanan usually composed his editorials standing at the case box, hand-setting each letter and word as he went along. He was thus occupied on the morning of May 4, 1884, when a group of highly agitated Union Pacific shopmen burst in to announce that the railroad had just posted wage reductions of ten to twenty-five per cent and that the infuriated men had walked off their jobs. Could Buchanan tell them—they were not members of the Order or any union— how to organize a strike?

Thoughtfully, Buchanan set the last line of his editorial and then agreed to go to a nearby hall, where he would address the strikers.

Firmly taking control of the unruly gathering, he offered a resolution of solidarity and got every man present to sign it. Notices were sent to shopmen along the entire railroad, and by the following day, a Friday, workers were out on strike from Ogden, Utah, to Omaha, Nebraska. The railroad buckled, and the wage cuts promptly were recalled.

With the taste of such a victory in their mouths, the Union Pacific shopmen rushed to form local assemblies of the Knights of Labor. The following August the Union Pacific again tried to cut wages and summarily dismissed men active in the May strike. The new Knights again struck, and Buchanan again forced the railroad to capitulate.

The two Union Pacific strikes marked the first time that a labor organization was able to deal with a giant corporation on terms of equality. At the 1884 General Assembly of the Knights of Labor, Buchanan was made a member of the Order's executive board.

In 1885 the Knights of Labor, guided once more by Buchanan, won their greatest victory—against the formidable power of Jay Gould, the financier and stock market speculator known as the Wizard of Wall Street.

In June the Wabash—one of the network of railroads controlled by Gould—closed its shops to members of the Order. The Knights on other Gould roads promptly petitioned the executive board for permission to call a sympathy strike. With Powderly ailing, Buchanan took control of the situation.

Buchanan had hoped to see A. A. Talmadge, general manager of the Wabash, but the railroad executive had left St. Louis on the very day that the Order's board assembled there. Irritated by what they considered management's rebuff, the board called a strike on the Wabash and asked workers on connecting railroads not to handle Wabash rolling stock. Then they set out after Talmadge, who was heading East to confer with Gould.

"We were doing our best to have a 'little talk' with the general manager of the Wabash," Buchanan wryly commented, "but he was too fleet-footed for us; besides he was making the itinerary—and keeping it to himself. . . ."

The chase ended, Buchanan reported, in Jay Gould's Manhattan office. Powderly, rapidly recovering, joined the group—it seems that he was rather flattered to be meeting on what appeared to be equal terms with the famed Wizard. To the obvious surprise of the board, Gould agreed to readmit the locked-out Knights.

The meeting concluded on a happy note, and labor and management parted as the best of friends. Subsequently, Powderly agreed that no further strikes would be called by

THE WALL STREET BLUEBEARD.
JAY GOULD, (*to* RESCUING BROTHER FELLOWS). — Who's afraid of *you?*

This savage comment on his way of operating railroads for profit alone pictures Jay Gould as "The Wall Street Bluebeard," about to lop off the head of the Missouri Pacific despite the timid admonition of a government prosecutor. At the rear are heads of his other "wives."

the Knights unless his new friends, the railroad executives, were informed in advance. In the meantime, this triumph marked the beginning of the phenomenal growth of the Knights of Labor.

The Knights of Labor that Powderly inherited from Uriah Stephens in 1879 claimed 20,151 members. By 1883, the Order had grown to 51,914. In July, 1885, the organization first claimed more than 100,000 members; but in the succeeding twelve months the membership increased more than sevenfold. On July 1, 1886, the Knights of Labor claimed that its following had swelled to an incredible 729,677.

A few years earlier, Jay Gould

successfully had broken a strike of telegraph operators on his railroads and forced the strikers back to work on his own terms. By giving in to the Knights on the Wabash in 1885, it was soon clear, Gould was but biding his time.

On February 18, 1886, a foreman in Gould's Texas Pacific shops at Marshall, Texas, was laid off—apparently because he had just served as a delegate to a Knights of Labor conclave. When the railroad refused to arbitrate this disagreement, the Texas Pacific district assembly called a strike —and it soon spread to the entire Southwest system of Gould railways.

"Tell the world that men of the Gould Southwest system are on strike," a workers' broadside commanded. "We strike for justice to ourselves and our fellowmen everywhere."

The Knights of Labor in the Southwest, however, had badly overestimated their strength. In the Union Pacific and Wabash strikes, the shopmen had been well organized and had been supported by the trainmen. On the Southwest railroads unorganized workers outnumbered the Knights 48,000 to 3,000. Along the Gould system, men were ready to take the strikers' jobs.

At the end of March the district leader who had touched off the strike in Texas wrote in panic to Powderly: "Men are being starved, others assaulted, lives are in jeopardy and property is being destroyed. . . . we can't win."

Again rising from a sickbed, Powderly hastened to New York. His meeting with Jay Gould, held this time in the Wizard's home, was somewhat less cordial.

Gould charged that the Order's executive board had no power over its men; had not Powderly promised to notify management in advance of any strikes? The embarrassed Master Workman, knowing how weak the strike effort actually was, offered to call the men back to work if Gould would agree to arbitration. Gould was adamant: the men must go back to work; then he would talk.

Violence broke out along the Southwest system as workers vented their fury against management—and possibly against the powerless leadership of the Knights of Labor as well. Congress appointed an investigating committee, and citizens' groups pleaded for a settlement. Finally, on May 4, the executive board of the Order called off the strike.

The strikers regarded it as a capitulation, and on the western railroads the Knights of Labor soon was a discredited organization.

That same day, May 4, 1886, a dramatic and horrifying event occurred in Chicago and did incalculable harm to the Knights of Labor.

The troubles in Chicago had been brewing for some time, and curiously enough, they had their origin in a proclamation of a workers' group that had sprung up in opposition to the Knights of Labor.

Most of the national trade unions that had been organized before and just after the Civil War—in the time of William Sylvis—had failed to survive the panic of 1873 and the hard times that followed. But a few struggled on, and in 1881 these weakened unions formed an organization with the grandiose title of The Federation of Organized Trades and Labor Unions of the United States and Canada.

The ambitious Federation dwindled and expired by 1886. (As will be seen in the following chapter, however, the American Federation of Labor—even today America's largest and most important labor organization—was built from the wreckage of the FTLU.) At its 1885 meeting, however, the group defiantly called for a nationwide strike to achieve the eight-hour day and set May 1, 1886, as the day to launch it.

Powderly, opposed as ever to strikes, tried to quash the Federation's idea immediately. Addressing the 1885 General Assembly of the Knights of Labor, he declared that "the proposition to inaugurate a general strike for the establishment of the short-hour plan on the first of May, 1886, should be discountenanced by this body. . . . The date fixed is not a suitable one; the plan suggested to establish the system is not the proper one."

Despite the Master Workman's stern injunction, the idea caught on; all across the country, workingmen's groups—including many local and district assemblies of the Order—began making plans for the eight-hour strike.

Chicago was the center of agitation. By the end of April, 62,000 workers—more than half of them from the city's meat-packing yards—had announced that they were ready to strike.

On May 1, 1886, a Saturday, 190,000 workers across the country walked out in support of the eight-hour day; in the following days the number on strike grew to 340,000—making this by far the nation's largest strike to that date.

Parades, mass meetings, and interminable speeches by impassioned orators were the order of the day in Chicago. What might have been a holiday

In the inflamed atmosphere of Chicago during the eight-hour-day strike, minor clashes between police and strikers often were magnified by the popular press. At right is a contemporary engraving of a police van under attack from a mob estimated at 12,000. The notice of the fateful May 4 meeting at the Haymarket was printed in English and German, far right.

mood, however, had a grim resolution about it. Among the strike leaders were socialists and anarchists preaching the overthrow of the government and the establishment of a Utopian workingman's society. City officials began to worry that the situation would get out of hand, and policemen were put on stand-by alert.

Sunday was a relatively quiet day, but the demonstrations were renewed on Monday, May 3. At a plant of the McCormick Harvester Company a scuffle broke out between strikers and the scabs hired to replace them. As policemen reached the scene, someone fired. One worker fell dead and five or six others were seriously wounded. One of the witnesses was August Spies, editor of a radical German-language newspaper. Rushing to his newspaper office, Spies composed an indignant and fiery broadside:

REVENGE! WORKINGMEN! TO ARMS! Your masters sent out their bloodhounds—the police—they killed six of your brothers at McCormick's this afternoon. . . . They killed them because they dared ask for the shortening of the hours of toil. . . .
If you are men, . . . rise . . . and destroy the hideous monster that seeks to destroy you. . . .

Hundreds of copies, in German as well as English, of this so-called Revenge Circular were distributed at labor meetings that evening.

By the following morning, Tuesday, May 4, a giant rally was being planned to protest police brutality. As an eyewitness to the McCormick

CULVER PICTURES

melee, August Spies was asked to be the chief speaker. Twenty thousand handbills announcing the meeting were passed out in Chicago: the time set, 7:30 P.M.; the place, the Haymarket.

In those days the Haymarket—a rectangular widening of Randolph Street between Halsted and Desplaines streets—was Chicago's largest outdoor public place. But when Spies arrived that evening, he was disappointed to see only a small crowd on hand.

Realizing that such an insignificant group—under 2,000—would be lost in the vast Haymarket, Spies led the people around the corner to an alleyway off Desplaines. From an improvised platform atop a wagon bed he called the meeting to order.

After a talk of some thirty minutes, Spies introduced Albert Parsons, editor of another radical newspaper.

Chicago's mayor, Carter Harrison, had lent his presence to the gathering, perhaps to guarantee that no one would disturb the peace. About half-way through Parsons' address the mayor withdrew, apparently satisfied that the situation was under control.

When Parsons finished talking at about 10 P.M., a third speaker, Samuel Fielden, rose and attempted to whip up some enthusiasm from the listless assembly:

"The socialists are not going to declare war; but I tell you war has been declared upon us; and I ask you to get hold of anything that will help to re-

sist the onslaught of the enemy. . . . What matters it whether you kill yourselves with work to get a little relief, or die on the battle field resisting the enemy?"

At this point, a cool wind blew in from Lake Michigan, dark rain clouds drifted over, and a light drizzle began falling. On the fringes of the crowd people started to wander off, and Parsons interrupted to suggest that they move indoors.

Suddenly, what was left of the crowd parted in surprise as a detachment of 180 police marching in close formation drew up to the wagon. "In the name of the people of the State of Illinois," the officer in charge said, "I command this meeting immediately and peaceably to disperse."

"We are peaceable," Fielden replied, as he turned to get down from the wagon.

Out of the darkness a sputtering bomb came hurtling, dropped to the ground in the front rank of the police column, and burst with a roar and a flash. After a moment of horrified silence, the police began firing, and the crowd, screaming in panic, fled.

One policeman was killed instantly; six more were fatally wounded; seventy officers suffered lesser wounds. Newspapers reported that one civilian had been killed and twelve wounded by police fire, but rumors circulated that sixty to seventy civilians actually had been injured.

Chicago and later the entire country was outraged by the bombing.

An emotional and somewhat inaccurate version of the Haymarket affair shows a bearded orator shouting as police and laborers exchange shots. The bomb is bursting in the background.

"Now It Is Blood!" shrieked the headline of the Chicago *Inter Ocean* the next morning. "It is now seen that the deadly bomb of Tuesday night was the logical and legitimate result of the red flag of a few days previous," a later edition of the paper reported in an attempt to link the bomb to the eight-hour strike.

Powderly hastened to disassociate the Knights of Labor from the Haymarket affair.

"The scenes of bloodshed and disorder which have occurred in Chicago are disgraceful, uncalled for, and deserving of the severest condemnation and punishment. Honest labor is not to be found in the ranks of those who march under the red flag of anarchy...."

Within days Spies, Fielden, and several other well-known anarchists and socialists were arrested and charged with the murder of the first police officer. Parsons, after first fleeing to Wisconsin, returned to give himself up on the day the trial opened, June 21. But the man accused of throwing the bomb, Rudolph Schnaubelt, never was brought to trial.

In the two-month-long Chicago trial it became evident that the men were being prosecuted for their radical beliefs. No convincing evidence ever was offered to connect any of them with the fatal bomb. Nevertheless, the jury, after a deliberation of only a few hours, found all of them guilty; one man, Oscar Neebe, was given fifteen years in prison; the other seven were sentenced to death.

A year of appeals followed the sentencing, and on the day before the scheduled execution the governor of Illinois—in response to a plea for clemency—commuted to life imprisonment the death sentences of Fielden and Michael Schwab. That very morning a third man, Louis Lingg, cheated the executioner by blowing off his head with a small bomb he somehow had rigged in his cell. On November 11, 1887, Spies, Parsons, Adolph Fischer, and George Engel were hanged.

Only in succeeding years did people come to see the injustice of executing these men—not for a crime of violence, which it never was proved that

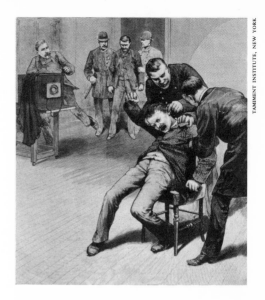

One of the men charged with the Haymarket explosion tries to resist the police photographer (above). "There will come a time," August Spies cried from the scaffold on which he and three others were about to be hanged (below), "when our silence will be more powerful than the voices you strangle today!" And indeed, the four were long regarded as martyrs of the labor movement.

60

they had committed, but rather for expressing their opinions, however radical. In June, 1893, a new governor of Illinois, John P. Altgeld, released the three men still imprisoned and pardoned the other five posthumously.

The Haymarket affair, despite Powderly's denunciation of the anarchists' violence, did irreparable harm to the entire labor movement.

"I'm not afraid of anarchy," a Chicago businessman said just before the executions. "Oh, no; it's the utopian scheme of a few, a *very* few, philosophizing cranks, who are amiable withal, but I do consider that the *labor movement should be crushed*! The Knights of Labor will never dare to create discontent again if these men are hanged."

During the summer and autumn of 1886 many of the gains won in the eight-hour strike were quickly wiped out as employers recalled their grants of a shorter day. And although the Knights of Labor membership was at its height, the Order already was showing signs of internal decay.

"It seemed last March and April as though the Golden Age were at hand," one labor editor sadly noted, "and now it seems as though [the workingmen have] been deceived by a will-o'-the-wisp."

Up to this point many of the national trade unions had maintained a tenuous relationship with the Knights of Labor simply because so many of their members also were Knights. Powderly now decided that these rival groups were a threat to the Order and his control of it. At the 1886 General Assembly he succeeded in having members of the large and quarrelsome Cigar Makers Union thrown out of the Order. Re-elected to a two-year term at an annual salary of $5,000, Powderly still was master of the Knights of Labor.

Even Powderly was alarmed at some of the claims made for him and the Order. Perhaps the most noteworthy was one in the hostile *New York Sun:*

Five men in this country control the chief interests of five hundred thousand workingmen, and can at any moment take the means of livelihood from two and a half millions of souls. These men compose the executive board of the noble order of the Knights of Labor. . . .

They can stay the nimble touch of almost every telegraph operator, can shut up most of the mills and factories, and can disable the railroads. They can issue an edict against any manufactured goods so as to make their subjects cease buying them, and the tradesmen stop selling them.

Of course, such an exaggerated description of the Order's power served only to make the large body of Americans fearful and suspicious of all labor organizations, especially in the wake of the Haymarket affair.

At the 1887 General Assembly, held in Minneapolis, Powderly—increasingly jealous of his power—succeeded in ousting Buchanan from the Knights. A later reconciliation attempted to patch up their differences, but Buchanan remained critical:

TWO ROADS FOR THE WORKINGMAN. ONE LEADS

To some Americans, including the artist who drew the cartoon above, the Knights of Labor and its
rival trade unions were runaway wagons on the "Road of Lawlessness and Disorder." On the other

RATIONAL ORGANISATION.

BROTHERHOOD OF LOCOMOTIVE ENGINEERS.

"I believe that in these labor troubles the only true remedy is that suggested by St. Paul: 'Come, let us reason together.' I hold that capital has rights that labor is bound to respect. * * I am opposed, decidedly opposed, to the means of coercion and violence to which some labor organizations resort. I hold that we have no right to detain a man from working for his family. We have a right to persuade * * * but beyond that we have no right to go. I believe that neglect of these principles by some labor organizations has brought a stigma upon honest labor that it will take years of honest labor to efface."—Chief Arthur.

HOME CLUB.

KNIGHTS OF LABOR.

POLITICAL INTRIGUE

J. KEPPLER

OSPERITY, AND THE OTHER TO VIOLENCE AND RUIN.

Puck, AUGUST 25, 1886: PRINTS DIVISION, NEW YORK PUBLIC LIBRARY

hand, the railroad brotherhoods, which seldom went on strike and concerned themselves chiefly with such matters as retirement benefits, seemed to be "rational organizations" making orderly progress.

"Mr. Powderly was an able agitator and leader of sentiment in a large and general way, but . . . he was unable to specialize and was almost worthless when it came to following a definite policy."

A good deal of Powderly's energies in later years was spent on promoting "co-operation," a movement to establish worker-owned factories and businesses. But such Utopian schemes never caught on in America.

By 1890, the Knights of Labor—discredited by its failures and torn by dissension—had dropped to a membership of 100,000. The notion of organizing into one vast group skilled and unskilled workers of many trades was too advanced for its time.

Only a few years earlier, Powderly had complained of the burdens of office: "The position I hold is too big for any ten men. It is certainly too big for me and I am only too willing to hand it over at once to whoever may be selected."

At the 1893 General Assembly Powderly's offer to resign as Master

The story of the emperor's new clothes, in which dishonest tailors trick a ruler into believing that their imaginary cloth can be seen only by him, is recast here as a comment on the late-19th-century labor movement. Unscrupulous labor leaders like the two at left have convinced the American worker (under canopy) that their programs will help clothe his nakedness.

Workman at first was rejected by the delegates. Still complaining, he again offered to resign—but this time, to his obvious surprise, the delegates turned to other leaders. After fourteen years Terence Powderly's career as chief of the Knights of Labor abruptly was ended.

The new leadership tried to ally the vanishing Knights of Labor with a reform political party, but there was really no Order left to lead. No reliable membership figures are available for the years after 1893, although officers continued to be elected well into the twentieth century.

Following his ouster as Master Workman, Powderly anxiously cast about for a new career. He sought a job as a conductor on the railroad for which he once had worked as machinist but was turned down. Rather courageously, at the age of forty-four, he returned to the study of law and was admitted to practice.

One of the influential friends Powderly had made in earlier days was William McKinley, then a Congressman from Ohio. When McKinley was inaugurated as President of the United States in 1897, Powderly secured from him appointment as Commissioner-General of Immigration. He retained this post until 1903, when he was relieved by Theodore Roosevelt for creating friction in the department. Later reinstated in government service, Powderly held several minor posts in the Immigration Service and in the Department of Labor until his death,

Making a pun on Terence Powderly's name, a cartoonist showed the leader of the Knights perched on a powder keg in danger of being ignited by a rail strike's red-hot irons.

at the age of 75, on January 24, 1924.

In 1917, between his government duties, Powderly was drafting his autobiography as a vindication of his controversial role in the labor movement. Elsewhere in Washington that year a man named John W. Hayes, the last Master Workman of the Knights of Labor, was gathering up all the remaining records and property of the once-mighty Order. One day he dragged all these belongings out to a leaky shed behind an insurance office, stored them inside, and put a final padlock on the Order of the Knights of Labor.

4

SAM GOMPERS' QUEST

The men worked sitting on hard benches at long, low tables. Their fingers moved swiftly, deftly, as they sorted the large brown tobacco leaves into bunches, then shaped, rolled, and cut them to form the blunt, firm cigars that were so popular in nineteenth-century America. In the dingy, poorly ventilated rooms in which New York's cigarmakers so often worked, a seat near the light and air of a door or window was greatly prized. Yet curiously enough, these seats did not always go to a senior worker, or to one most highly skilled; instead the place of honor often was given to a man who was not actually working with his hands that day.

The apparently inactive worker was the reader or group discussion leader. A skilled trade that required some practice to achieve proficiency, cigarmaking—once mastered—was a mechanical function. Working only with their hands, the men in the city's

Helping to organize the A.F. of L., Samuel Gompers visited strike-torn West Virginia coal mines—and struck the nonchalant pose at left for a suspicious detective's camera.

numerous small shops and factories found their minds free during the interminable hours of toil. And thus, as the men about him worked furiously, one of their number—paid by the others out of their own earnings—would read to the others and draw them out in discussion about what was read. The subjects invariably discussed were politics and unions.

Some of the most intense and thoughtful discussions took place at the cigarmaking shop operated by David Hirsch on Lower Manhattan's Chambers Street. One young man employed at Hirsch's in 1873 was destined to be America's foremost unionist of the next half-century.

Samuel Gompers was twenty-three when he went to work for David Hirsch. Born in London of a Dutch-Jewish family, he had come to the United States in 1863 with his immigrant parents. In New York his father continued to work at the cigarmaking that had been his trade in England. Laboring at home—a dreary tenement between a slaughterhouse and a brewery—the senior Gompers immediately set thirteen-year-old Sam to making cigars, too. Like other immigrants, the Gompers had hoped to find a better life in America, but it seemed as though they merely had exchanged the drabness of London's East End for the poverty of New York's East Side.

As in other decades and in other trades, the cigarmakers' union—of which Sam and his father soon were members—seemed to flourish in good times and decline in hard times. The year Samuel Gompers went to work for David Hirsch, 1873, marked the beginning of a four-year-long depression, and Hirsch's soon was the only union shop left in New York.

In later years Gompers was to describe the "little forum" at Hirsch's as the best education he ever received. Most of the men in the shop were German, but Gompers soon picked up enough of the language to follow their conversations. He read Karl Marx's *Communist Manifesto* and other works on socialism and later joined an evening discussion group.

"In those young days I was full of fire and dreams and burning with sentiment," Gompers later wrote, "and I might have followed any course or associated myself with any movement that seemed to promise freedom for my pals and fellow-workers."

The depression deepened toward the end of 1873, and the onset of winter brought increased suffering to New York's unemployed workers. "Christmas in New York was not festive that year," Gompers recalled.

Early in the New Year unemployed workers planned a mass protest and set the morning of January 13 at the Lower East Side's Tompkins Square as the time and place for their gathering. Official permission to hold the meeting was granted, and the mayor promised to come and address the workers.

Sam Gompers, among the first to arrive that morning, uneasily noted that a sizable police detachment surrounded the park. Half an hour later, a large workers' group carrying a banner labeled "Tenth Ward Union Labor" marched into Tompkins Square from Avenue A. "Without a word of warning," Gompers wrote, "[the police] swept down upon the defenseless workers, striking down the standard-bearer and using their clubs right and left indiscriminately on the heads of all they could reach."

The terrified protesters fled the park and scurried down Eighth Street, closely pursued by the mounted police. Caught in the melee, Sam just missed being cracked on the skull by jumping into an open cellarway.

This ugly outburst of police brutality taught Samuel Gompers a life-long lesson: radical protest would serve only to direct the fury of organized society against labor. Progress in the labor movement must be slow and orderly.

One of the older men at Hirsch's also had cautioned the impressionable Sam Gompers about radical philosophies, such as socialism and anarch-

Demonstrating workers are sent fleeing by a mounted policeman in this contemporary engraving of the 1874 Tompkins Square melee. Depicting the workers as brutes, the artist betrayed his antagonism to them. Papers referred to "riotous communist workingmen."

ism. "Study your union card, Sam," he would say whenever young Gompers advanced some new theory he had just read about, "and if the idea doesn't square with that, it ain't true."

Unfortunately, outside of Hirsch's shop, there were not many New York cigarmakers even holding union cards. Combined membership of the city's two locals had stood at a mere 131 at the end of 1872. That year a dynamic cigarmaker named Adolph Strasser arrived from Hungary and began to revitalize the union.

Progress in organizing the cigarmakers was discouragingly slow. Not until November, 1875, were the fragmented New York workers granted a new charter by the Cigarmakers International Union. Officers of this new group—Local 144—included Samuel Gompers, president, and Adolph Strasser, financial secretary. Two years later, Strasser captured the presidency

of the International, and together he and Gompers created an efficient union that served as a model for the entire American labor movement.

The Cigarmakers faced their greatest challenge in 1877. At the end of four years of depression the United States was experiencing unprecedented industrial unrest, with long and often violent strikes from coast to coast. Strasser and Gompers set out to organize the most miserable of New York's cigarmakers, the tenement-house workers who, though leaderless, had gone on strike.

These wretched folk, most of them non-English-speaking immigrants, worked endless hours in their own homes—cramped, dingy apartments in tenement buildings, some owned by the cigar manufacturers themselves. Father, mother, and children from age five or six up worked furiously from dawn to late in the evening. They

Four members of an immigrant family turn a corner of their dingy apartment into a cigarmaking plant.

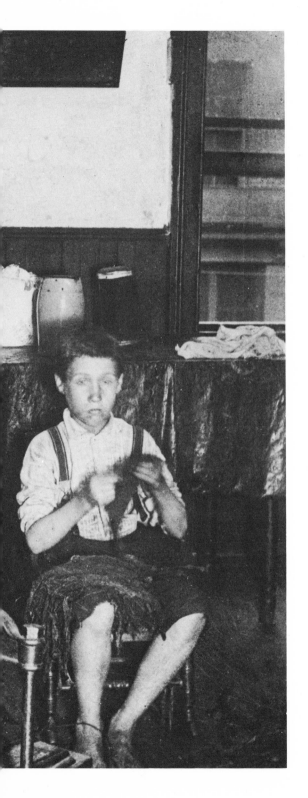

scarcely paused to eat, and falling exhausted each night into bed, slept fitfully only to rise and begin the depressing cycle again the next day. In hard times they generally lost not only their work but their quarters as well, when the tenement owners evicted them without warning.

The CIU opened soup kitchens for the striking tenement workers and tried to find lodgings for those evicted. Gompers and other skilled workers who still were employed helped support the strikers, and the union men finally set up a co-operative cigarmaking shop to employ those without work. Gompers left his $18-a-week job to run this union enterprise for $12.

At last the manufacturers locked out the skilled workers as well. Slowly the strike disintegrated, and by early 1878, the defeated workers were straggling back to work. The co-operative was closed down, but as a blacklisted strike leader Gompers could not find work elsewhere.

With one child ill and his wife, Sophia, expecting another baby any day, Gompers took to roaming the city—his tools of trade in hand—looking for employment. Soon everything was pawned except Sophia's wedding ring. Sam got five dollars for his heavy winter coat that spring, then back at work at last, he spent all summer trying to save money to reclaim the coat when he would need it.

Strasser had set up a little office for the CIU on Chatham Street, and often Gompers would drop in after work to discuss union business. As darkness approached, Strasser would lock up and the two men would set out to walk home, still engaged in animated conversation. Arriving at Gompers' doorstep, they usually would stand talking for some minutes more, then move unconsciously off toward Strasser's house. Occasionally they would pass half the night walking back and forth between their residences, not wishing to stop talking about unions long enough to say good night.

The two cigarmakers insisted on absolute control of strikes by the CIU and the steady accumulation of strike funds by all locals. They also established the principle whereby a prosperous, working local would transfer funds to a weak, striking body. By 1881, the CIU claimed 12,709 members and was one of America's most powerful and efficient unions.

For some years Gompers had been meeting informally with representatives of other unions, principally the carpenters and tailors. Although many trade union leaders also were Knights of Labor, they were beginning to fear that the influx of so many unskilled workers into the Order threatened their organizations of skilled workers. "Pure and simple trade unionism," was the gospel as preached by Gompers and his circle. Higher wages, shorter hours, and better working conditions were their aim.

To promote trade unionism in America, they felt, a national organi-zation was needed—a group with goals quite different from those of the Utopian Knights of Labor. Yet since the disappearance of William Sylvis' National Labor Union in 1872, there had been no such national association of trade unions.

The International Typographical Union was an early advocate of national federation, and in 1881 the ITU's corresponding secretary issued a call for a conference of trade unions. Only twenty-one delegates attended that first meeting, but a second conference, on November 15, 1881, at Pittsburgh, turned out to be a more auspicious affair.

Of the 107 delegates, nearly half represented Knights of Labor assemblies, but the rest were dedicated trade unionists. At the gathering the ambitious Federation of Organized Trades and Labor Unions of the United States and Canada was launched.

The following year Gompers became chairman of the new group.

Just thirty-two, Gompers was among the nation's youngest labor leaders. He was a conspicuously short man, scarcely five feet four inches tall. Although his legs were stumpy, he had a well-developed torso, with a barrel chest and lungs that were the source of his deep, booming voice. To disguise a youthful appearance, he had affected a drooping walrus mustache and a tiny goatee.

The Federation never caught on, and by 1884, only the cigarmakers and typographers were giving it any real support. Undaunted, the delegates at the next year's convention made their brave call for a general strike to establish the eight-hour day beginning May 1, 1886.

The 1886 eight-hour-day strike led —as we have seen—to the Haymarket Affair.

"The effect of that bomb," Gompers stated, "was that it not only killed the policemen, but it killed our eight-hour movement for that year and for a few years just after, notwithstanding we had absolutely no connection with these people."

The dispute between the Knights of Labor and the trade unions also was coming to a head. Since 1881 there had been a division in the ranks of New York's cigarmakers, one group following Strasser and Gompers, the other favoring Terence Powderly's Knights. Ideological differences led to personal antagonisms; Powderly, a teetotaler, once complained that he never had seen the convivial Sam Gompers sober. The dispute reached a climax at the September, 1886, General Assembly of the Knights, when cigarmakers who insisted on belonging also to the CIU were thrown unceremoniously out of the Order.

Almost immediately, Strasser, along with leaders of the iron and steel workers, iron molders, carpenters, and mineworkers' unions called for a trade union convention, December 8, 1886, at Columbus, Ohio. The stage thus was set for the formation of the United States' most enduring labor organization.

Forty-two delegates representing twenty-five unions with a total membership of 317,000 workers met at Columbus to establish the American Federation of Labor. Sam Gompers was unanimously elected first president of the A.F. of L. and given the sum of $160.52 to set up a national headquarters in New York.

The A.F. of L.'s first office was a single room on East Eighth Street— not far from the cellar where Sam had hidden from the police during the Tompkins Square melee thirteen years earlier. Gompers furnished this room with the family's kitchen table and a box for the president to sit on. His daughter Rose contributed a child's writing desk, which was nailed to the wall so that an adult could work at it, and his son Henry scavenged used tomato crates from a nearby grocer for filing cases.

From this modest office Gompers sent an endless stream of letters to unions around the country, quietly yet forcefully presenting the arguments for joining the A.F. of L. At the second annual convention, in 1887, the iron and steel workers, brewers, and glassworkers' unions federated, bringing the membership up to 600,000. Within one year the A.F. of L. had eclipsed the declining Knights of Labor. More important for Sam Gompers was the fact that dues paid by the affiliates amounted to $2,100.34— enough to pay his annual salary of

$1,000 and even leave money for important organizing work.

In years to come, under Gompers' leadership, the A.F. of L. created national unions out of local trade groups, organized such trades as the teamsters and garment workers, and settled jurisdictional disputes between rival unions. Throughout the A.F. of L.'s history, affiliated unions have stoutly maintained their independence, and Gompers always was careful to explain that as president of the Federation he could only suggest and persuade but not force member unions to take certain courses of action. Nevertheless, his cautious approach often achieved dramatic results.

THE AMERICAN WORKINGMAN OF THE FUTURE.
When the Labor Agitators Have "Improved His Condition" Until He is Perfectly Satisfied With It.

Unions, this 1887 cartoon warned, were giving workers the notion that they might someday compose essays, visit Europe, take up sports, enter Congress, and even mingle in society.

Rather than call another general strike for the eight-hour day, Gompers suggested that one union at a time seek the shorter day. On May 1, 1890, the carpenters—backed with a fund raised by assessing all other trade union members two cents each —demanded, and won, the eight-hour day. But the following year, plans to use the same tactics for mineworkers fell through.

The year 1892 brought the Homestead tragedy described in Chapter 1. Gompers visited the beleaguered steel town to tell the strikers that "the hearts of the American people beat in unison and in sympathy" for them, and the A.F. of L. contributed $7,000 in strike relief.

Gompers' moderate leadership was not admired by one vocal group, the socialists, and in the early 1890's they began snapping at his heels. At the 1894 A.F. of L. convention, delegates were offered a new labor platform. Plank ten called for collective ownership by the people of all means of production and distribution in the United States—a clear call to replace American capitalism with socialism.

The radical plank was defeated, but Gompers' triumph in turning back the socialists was short-lived.

Thwarted on the platform, many of the radical delegates—including some from his own cigarmakers' union—turned against Gompers and elected John McBride of the United Mine Workers to the presidency, by a vote of 1,170 to 976.

The next year was Sam Gompers' "sabbatical" from the Federation, and he spent most of the year plotting a return to office. McBride soon became too ill to devote full time to the presidency, and at the 1895 convention Gompers defeated his re-election bid by eighteen votes. The following year, 1896, however, Gompers was unanimously re-elected—as he would be for many years to come; his hold on the A.F. of L. thereafter was a firm one.

The socialists continued to attack Gompers in private and in public at the annual conventions. A spellbinding orator, Sam found no subject more enticing than an attack on his enemies, the socialists. As he would launch into one of his famous sarcastic broadsides, enthusiastic supporters would jump to their feet, crying, "Give 'em hell, Sam; give 'em hell."

At the 1896 convention that unanimously re-elected Gompers, the Federation's headquarters was shifted to Washington, D.C., where Sam and the other officers would be in a better position to present labor's demands to the federal government.

The American Federation of Labor, and Samuel Gompers, were becoming respectable. In Washington Gompers was received cordially by President William McKinley, who listened patiently to the labor leader's problems. During the administration of McKinley's successor, Theodore Roosevelt, Sam became an even more frequent visitor to the White House.

At one session with the President, Gompers pressed his case relentlessly, almost rudely. Exasperated, Roosevelt said: "But I am President of the United States." Gompers shot back: "And I, sir, am president of the American Federation of Labor."

In 1901 Gompers joined the National Civic Federation, a supposedly impartial body of public-spirited citizens who would help to arbitrate labor disputes. He soon was conferring with such dignitaries as former President Cleveland, Archbishop Ireland, Senator Marcus Hanna, and John D. Rockefeller, Jr. Criticized for joining this conservative-minded group, Gompers answered that he would "appeal to the devil, or to his mother-in-law, to help Labor, if Labor could be aided in that way."

In 1902 the A.F. of L., for the first time, claimed a membership of over one million men. And a strike that year in northeastern Pennsylvania's anthracite coal region gave dramatic evidence that organized labor was at last a force in the land.

Four years earlier, in 1898, twenty-eight-year-old John Mitchell had become president of the United Mine Workers. Although the UMW had succeeded in organizing the bituminous coal miners from western Pennsylvania to Illinois, the union—one of the A.F. of L.'s largest affiliates—had made no progress with the anthracite workers. Mitchell, a slim but muscular young man, took on the job of organizing the anthracite miners.

Many of the coal miners about Scranton and Wilkes-Barre were recent immigrants, easily exploited by the railroad companies that controlled the mines. They had to dig 2,800 to 3,190 pounds of coal to get paid for a ton; they had to pay the company $2.75 for a keg of blasting powder worth $1.10; and they often were paid in scrip that could be spent only in company-owned stores charging unusually high prices.

By mid-1900, Mitchell had succeeded in getting 9,000 of the area's some 150,000 anthracite miners to join the UMW. Yet that September he called a strike that finally was joined by some ninety per cent of the workers. This was a presidential election year, however, and Senator Hanna persuaded the employers to grant a ten per cent wage increase. Hanna's action ended the strike, thus insuring a supply of coal during the winter and avoiding embarrassment to President McKinley's re-election campaign.

The mine owners, however, refused to recognize the union and guaranteed only that the increased wages would remain in effect until April 1, 1901. On that date, again without acknowledging existence of the union, the employers extended the wage agreement for one year.

When April 1, 1902, came and went, Mitchell tried in vain to get the owners to confer with the UMW.

Finally, on May 15, the anthracite coal miners voted to strike, and some 150,000 workers walked out. Refus-

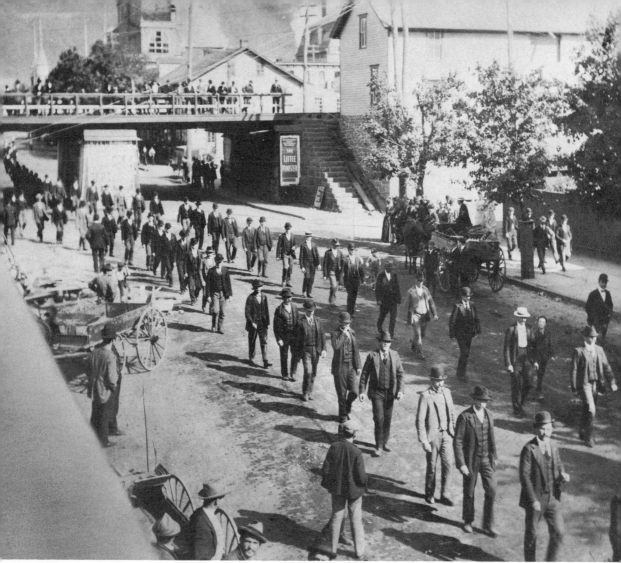

Anthracite coal miners on strike in 1902 don their Sunday finest for this orderly march through Shenandoah, Pennsylvania. At left, a bespectacled Theodore Roosevelt betrays his sympathies by posing congenially with some of the strikers. The men cannot conceal their pride in the President's reassuring visit.

77

An 1899 certificate of membership in the United Mine Workers was framed by scenes from a miner's life. Union initiation is shown at top; below is a glamorized version of his workday.

ing a sympathy strike, the better-organized bituminous workers stayed on the job—and eventually helped to raise a strike fund of $2,500,000 for their less fortunate brothers. Nevertheless, by late summer, the situation was desperate.

Thousands of unemployed workers climbed aboard freight trains, "Johnny Mitchell specials," to leave the stricken area, and the Pennsylvania National Guard was called out when violence erupted at several points.

George Baer, Jr., president of the Philadelphia and Reading Coal and Iron Company, unwittingly caused much of the public to side with the strikers when a letter of his was published in the press. "The rights and interests of the laboring man," the industrialist had written, "will be protected and cared for, not by the labor agitator, but by the Christian men to whom God in his infinite wisdom has given the control of the property interests of the country."

In early October an exasperated Theodore Roosevelt summoned both sides to a Washington conference. The dynamic and emotional President scarcely could keep his temper as the mine owners asked him to "do his duty" and suppress the strike. Polite and serious, Mitchell impressed Roosevelt more than all the employers put together.

At last the operators agreed to submit the dispute to a commission—if the President appointed its members subject to their approval. They wanted a military man, a federal judge, a mining engineer, a businessman familiar with the anthracite industry, and finally an "eminent sociologist." There was no place whatsoever on the commission for a union leader.

In dismay, Roosevelt scanned the list; then suddenly he found an amusing way to get around the mine owners. As a sociologist he picked E. E. Clark, Grand Chief of the Order of Railway Conductors, "a man who has thought and studied deeply on social questions and has practically applied his knowledge."

Meeting in Scranton and Philadelphia over the next four months, the commission heard 558 witnesses, called by both sides in the dispute, and made its award early in 1903. For the period from April 1, 1903, to April 1, 1906, a ten-per-cent wage increase was to be granted the coal miners, an eight-hour day was to be established for most workers, and the miners could have their own representatives check to see if they were getting fair measurement of their coal. Most important of all, the United Mine Workers was recognized as the workers' spokesman.

With the successful intervention in a labor dispute by the President of the United States for the first time, organized labor, the A.F. of L., and Sam Gompers seemed headed for greater triumphs. Three unfortunate events of the next few years dashed nearly all their high hopes.

In 1890 Congress had passed the Sherman Anti-Trust Act, aimed at curbing the giant corporations that were coming to dominate American business life. Soon, however, the courts were issuing injunctions against strikes, claiming the unions were, in effect, corporations of workers acting to restrain trade.

In 1902 the United Hatters Union tried to win a closed, or all-union, shop agreement from Loewe and Company of Danbury, Connecticut. When their strike failed, the hatters instituted a boycott of the firm's products that cost the company close to $100,000 in lost sales.

Loewe and Company promptly sued under terms of the Sherman Act, carrying its case all the way to the Supreme Court. In 1908 the high court ruled that the boycott was an illegal restraint of trade and a lower court then awarded the hat manufacturer damages of $252,000. All the savings and even the homes of the Danbury hatters could be seized to pay the award.

"The rights of hats seem to be greater than the rights of man," Gompers fumed in *The American Federationist*, the official A.F. of L. publication. The Federation already had paid court costs of nearly $100,000 and immediately set out to raise, from other unions, the money needed to save the threatened hatters.

By this time, Gompers himself was in trouble over another court case. A St. Louis industrialist named James

Van Cleave had helped form the National Association of Manufacturers, a group openly hostile to labor organizations. Van Cleave's firm, the Buck's Stove and Range Company, naturally refused to negotiate with union workers. Buck's Stove thereupon was added to the firms included in *The American Federationist*'s "We Don't Patronize" list.

In 1907 Van Cleave got a court injunction preventing the A.F. of L. from listing his firm in its publication. In an editorial Gompers exploded: "Until a law is passed making it compulsory upon labor men to

buy Van Cleave's stoves we need not buy them, we won't buy them, and we will persuade other fair-minded, sympathetic friends of labor to co-operate with us and leave the blamed things alone. Go to——with your injunctions."

Gompers and other A.F. of L. officials were summoned before a District of Columbia judge and charged with contempt of court. The threat of huge fines and prison terms hung over their heads for the next few years, until the United States Supreme Court finally dismissed the case on a technicality.

In a demonstration of labor solidarity, Sam Gompers journeyed to Los Angeles to visit the two McNamara brothers in jail and pose for the above photograph. The A.F. of L. chieftain offered to help defend the two ironworkers against the charge of dynamiting the Los Angeles Times. *At left, workers poke in the debris the morning after the blast.*

Another uncompromising opponent of organized labor in those years was General Harrison Grey Otis, publisher of the Los Angeles *Times*. The *Times* building was constructed like a medieval fortress, Otis rode about town with a small cannon mounted on his automobile, and Los Angeles—under his leadership—was the nation's largest open shop, or nonunion, city.

Early on the morning of October 1, 1910, the *Times* building was blown up, with a loss of twenty-one lives. Some investigators blamed leaking gas pipes for the explosion, but Otis immediately charged that it was the work of left-wing union agitators. The following April detectives burst into a board meeting of the International Bridge and Structural Iron Workers Union in Indianapolis and seized the union's secretary-treasurer, John J. McNamara. Along with his brother, James B. McNamara, the union official was charged with the *Times* dynamiting.

Across the country union men screamed that this was a frame-up. The two McNamaras were extradited to California to face trial, and Gompers hastened to their side, to be photographed with them in jail as he pledged the full support of the A.F. of L.

Gompers was en route to New York on union business on December 1, 1911, when two reporters came aboard the train to say that the McNamaras, at the opening of their trial in Los Angeles, had pleaded guilty.

Newsmen hounded Gompers around New York during the next few days, trying to learn if he and the A.F. of L. also were implicated in the dynamiting. Gompers stoutly denied any knowledge of the brothers' guilt. Linking him personally to confessed criminals, the McNamara case shocked Gompers perhaps more than anything else in his long career.

Fortunately for Sam Gompers and the A.F. of L., the next year— 1912—was a presidential election year, and the Democratic nominee, Woodrow Wilson, turned out to be a friend of labor.

What did he want for American labor? Gompers often was asked. "More!" was his simple but forceful answer. In 1906 the A.F. of L. had spelled out what that "more" was, in a list called Labor's Bill of Grievances. The demands included extension of the eight-hour day; protection from competition of convict labor; exclusion of Chinese and restriction of other immigration, which was bringing cheap labor to American shores; protection of the rights of seamen; exemption of labor from the antitrust laws; and abolition of the use of court injunctions in labor disputes. Yet by 1912, when Woodrow Wilson was nominated, labor's grievances still had not been redressed.

Under Gompers' leadership the Federation generally had avoided direct political action. Legislation could

A 1912 campaign button identified presidential candidate Wilson as a friend of labor.

not force management to grant labor's demands, he felt; the workingman's gains could be won only by collective bargaining between employer and employees. Wilson felt differently.

"The working people of America —if they must be distinguished from the minority that constitutes the rest of it—are, of course, the backbone of the nation," Wilson told the Democratic nominating convention. Legislation that protected their interest, he added, could scarcely be called "class legislation or anything but a measure taken in the interest of the whole people."

To his cabinet Woodrow Wilson appointed the first Secretary of Labor, William B. Wilson, no relation but a former secretary-treasurer of the United Mine Workers. And on October 15, 1914, the President signed into law the Clayton Act.

An updating of the Sherman Anti-Trust Act of 1890, the Clayton Act stated that "the labor of a human being is not a commodity or article of commerce." Labor unions no longer could be held "illegal combinations in restraint of trade." Strikes, picketing, and boycotts were recognized as legal actions, and finally, court injunctions could not be used in labor disputes unless it was decided that such injunctions were needed to prevent "irreparable injury to property." Thereafter, this last clause was cited to justify continued use of injunctions, but for a time it seemed as though organized labor had won an historic victory.

The Clayton Act, Gompers proudly asserted, was labor's Magna Charta. And later in Wilson's administration, laws were passed protecting seamen's rights and granting the eight-hour day to railroad trainmen.

In an 1894 labor dispute Gompers had sent a telegram to Grover Cleveland requesting the President's intervention. Cleveland had not even bothered to reply. By Woodrow Wilson's time, Gompers and the A.F. of L. had come a long way.

On the Fourth of July, 1916, the American Federation of Labor dedicated a grand new headquarters in Washington, and standing next to a beaming Sam Gompers was President Wilson himself. The following year Wilson traveled to Buffalo to address the annual A.F. of L. convention.

Wilson's appearance at the convention and his praise of Gompers there were not exactly a spontaneous gesture. The United States had just entered World War I, and the government needed the support of organized labor. Acting with great energy and

THE NEW OFFICER.

A 1914 cartoonist depicted the Clayton Anti-Trust Act as the new officer on the beat, ready to use a club marked "penalties" on trusts, represented by a top-hatted robber.

enthusiasm, Gompers got behind the President. He served as a member of the Council of National Defense and saw that labor disputes did not hinder the war effort. In 1918 he made a triumphant tour of Europe and visited the doughboys in the trenches.

As a reward for his wartime support, Gompers thoroughly expected to be named as an American delegate to the peace conference at Paris in 1919. Passed over by Wilson, Sam consoled himself with a lesser position: chairman of the Commission on International Labor Legislation, meeting simultaneously in Paris.

That year, 1919, was to witness a bitter defeat for labor in the United States and to mark the beginning of the decline of Sam Gompers' power.

Following its defeat at Homestead in 1892, the Amalgamated Association of Iron, Steel, and Tin Workers had gone into a long slump. In 1901 Carnegie's company had been merged into the giant U.S. Steel Corporation. Led by U.S. Steel, the major producers simply refused to recognize any union of steelworkers. Yet working conditions in the steel industry had changed little; men still worked grueling twelve-hour days, with an inhuman twenty-four-hour shift at the turn-over from night to day work every two weeks.

In 1918 twenty-four unions—A.F. of L. affiliates—formed a national organizing committee for the steel industry and dispatched organizers to the nation's principal steel areas. Although it soon was reported that men were flocking into the unions, the drive was hampered by the lack of funds and by a business slump.

Elbert H. Gary, chairman of U.S. Steel, politely but firmly declined to

In a violent incident of the 1919 steel strike, mounted police charge into a group of workers on a Philadelphia sidewalk. A few women are among those scurrying away from the billy clubs.

84

meet with members of the organizing committee. It was a well-known fact, he commented, that U.S. Steel did not recognize unions.

On September 22, 1919, the committee called a strike—and to its surprise and delight, the walkout was an almost complete success. Across the nation an estimated 360,000 steel workers stayed away from their jobs, double the number that actually had joined the various unions during the organizing drive. Yet the steel industry refused to give in.

The strike dragged on into late autumn. Mounted police intimidated pickets, and newspapers published erroneous information about strikers going back to work. So tight was company control of some steel towns that no outside organizers were allowed to stay overnight.

Rabbi Stephen Wise of New York asked if he could address Duquesne, Pennsylvania, workers. The mayor answered: "Jesus Christ himself could not speak in Duquesne for the A.F. of L.!"

By mid-December, the strike was faltering and in January, 1920, the organizing committee had to admit defeat. The unionization of the giant steel industry was yet another generation away.

That year the A.F. of L. reached a membership peak of just over four

Pittsburgh Chronicle Telegraph, OCTOBER, 1919: TAMIMENT INSTITUTE, NEW YORK

Defiant steelworkers (above, left) hold the strike announcement of September 22, 1919. The next month a paper showed Uncle Sam giving the back-to-work order in eight languages.

The collapse of the 1919 steel strike left the unorganized workers of that industry still awaiting improvement of their lot. Above, ramshackle houses line a drab street in Pittsburgh.

million, then went into a slow but steady decline. And Sam Gompers was beginning to lose his hold on the organization.

With his hair coming out in patches and his jowly chin sinking down on his short neck, Gompers in old age— a woman seeing him for the first time said—looked like "a grotesque frog." His favorite daughter had succumbed to influenza in 1918; his 92-year-old father passed away the next year; and in May, 1920, his beloved wife, Sophia, died. In 1919 Gompers was injured in a New York taxicab accident. He contracted diabetes and he grad-

ually began to lose his eyesight. By this time, Sam seemed to be interested only in remaining president of the A.F. of L. until his death. Yet at the 1921 convention he faced a serious threat to his leadership for the first time in years. After three decades of nearly automatic re-election to the presidency, Gompers saw John L. Lewis of the United Mine Workers capture a third of the votes.

Gompers nevertheless busied himself with ambitious schemes to organize Mexican and South American labor, and appropriately the 1924 convention was held at El Paso,

Texas. Delegates from the Mexican Federation of Labor meeting in Juarez were greeted at the International Bridge and escorted to the A.F. of L. meeting.

The old man had intended to play only a symbolic role at the convention, but he held the gavel throughout the long sessions. At his side sat an aide who whispered names into his ear when the nearly blind leader failed to recognize the voice of some delegate who wished to address the convention. His unanimous re-election to the presidency, for the last time, was a foregone conclusion.

Against the wishes of his doctors, Gompers left El Paso after the convention to attend the inauguration of Mexico's new president in Mexico City. The change of climate and high altitude, and the constant round of activities, at last proved too much for the aged Gompers. He collapsed and had to be carried to his train.

Life flickered in his body just long enough for him to return to American soil; at San Antonio, on December 13, 1924, Samuel Gompers died. He was six weeks short of his seventy-fifth birthday.

A special train took Sam Gompers' body back east. En route, labor men lined the tracks in silent tribute; governors and union leaders came aboard to pay their last respects. The flag-draped coffin was displayed at A.F. of L. headquarters in Washington and then was taken to New York for services and burial.

A dignified Sam Gompers poses aboard ship as he embarks on a trip to Europe.

Forty-three years earlier, he had reminded the delegates at El Paso, a group of trade unionists had met at Pittsburgh to establish the Federation that was the A.F. of L.'s immediate forerunner. He was the last survivor of that historic gathering.

Reviewing his decades of service to organized labor, he concluded: "We shall never stop. Some of us may and will pass over to the Great Beyond, but there are others who will rise and take our place and do as well, if not better than we have done."

For labor, the goal was still "More."

THE VANGUARD OF ANARCHY.

5

LABOR ON THE LEFT

Visitors from Europe, in the late 1880's, were directed to the Chicago suburb of Pullman—just as, a half-century earlier, other arrivals from abroad had been urged to inspect Lowell, Massachusetts. There on the flat prairies had been erected a model town for industrial workers.

"It is famous already as one of the wonders of the west," a Chicago newspaper boasted of Pullman in 1885. "Splendid provision has been made for the present comfort of its eight thousand residents [and] its four thousand workmen. . . . More completely and on a larger scale than was probably ever before attempted, there is seen here a sympathetic blending of the useful and the beautiful."

No one was more gratified by such praise than the town's founder, George M. Pullman. Only two decades earlier, Pullman had introduced the sleeping car that had revolutionized train travel in the United States.

A Harper's Weekly *cartoonist, commenting on the 1894 Pullman strike, depicted Eugene Debs as the king of anarchy, supported by Illinois Governor Altgeld as court jester.*

By 1894, Pullman sleeping cars would be used exclusively along three fourths of the nation's railway mileage.

As his firm expanded, George Pullman conceived the idea of building a model town that would consolidate most of the firm's workshops and dwellings for his employees in one place. Chicago, the railway hub of the nation, was the obvious location for such a town, and early in 1880 Pullman quietly bought up 4,000 acres of land twelve miles south of the Illinois metropolis. A noted architect, a landscape designer, engineers, and an army of workers converged on the site to build the town.

Paved streets with cobblestone gutters separated neat rows of brick tenement dwellings, while individual homes were set back on lawns behind tree-lined walks. An exuberant variety of Victorian architectural styles broke the monotony of the planned city.

Stores and offices of the company were housed in the Arcade, a huge structure named after the glass passage bisecting it. A church, a theatre, a library, a hotel, and a school also were provided, and a lovely park

bordered a man-made lake near the center of town.

To outsiders Pullman indeed seemed like a workers' paradise. All was uniform and harmonious; everything was regulated and predictable. Rent was deducted from the salary checks; food was purchased in company stores; books could be checked out of the company library.

Even at the outset, however, there were signs of discontent. Rent for the church proved so high that for several years the building stood vacant, and Roman Catholics were long denied a separate place of worship. Most workers could not afford the annual fee for library membership. One observer described the model town as a "civilized relic of European serfdom."

A Pullman worker once described his lot: "We are born in a Pullman house, fed from the Pullman shop, taught in the Pullman school, cate-chized in the Pullman church, and when we die we shall be buried in the Pullman cemetery and go to the Pullman hell."

Yet despite such occasional grumblings, life in Pullman proved tolerable, and for the times, perhaps even pleasant for most workers—as long as a prosperous America kept buying and using Pullman cars.

The fiscal year ending July 31, 1893, proved to be one of the most profitable in the company's history, but immediately thereafter—and without warning—new orders virtually halted. The United States just then was entering another of its periodic business depressions.

To secure even a few orders for new sleeping cars and for the other railway equipment he built, George Pullman that fall authorized a reduction in his prices of 25 per cent. And he asked that his workers share the

The engraving above, made in 1893, shows George Pullman's village—a supposedly harmonious town with factories, homes, and public buildings, all set on a man-made lake. It was Pullman (right) who perfected the convertible railroad sleeping car (below).

financial burden by accepting reduced wages. By April, 1894, some of Pullman's employees were earning 33 to 40 per cent less than they had a year earlier.

Although their wages plummeted, Pullman workers found themselves paying the same rents—already 20 to 25 per cent higher than those of Chicago. One skilled mechanic reported that his salary for two weeks—after the nine-dollar rent on his company house had been paid—was exactly $.07.

On May 7, 1894, a delegation of Pullman workers visited the corporation's offices to demand that wage cuts be restored or that rents be reduced. Told to return for an answer two days later, they were confronted by George Pullman himself.

The industrialist first offered to let the workers inspect the company books to see that falling profits made it necessary to cut wages. As for rents, he stated, there was no connection in his mind between construction of railway equipment and the Pullman company's real estate ventures. They were two separate enterprises.

The following day three members of the workers' grievance committee who had appeared before George Pullman were dismissed. Rumors had it that the company would shut down at noon on May 11. Rather than face such a lockout, the committee called a strike, and three thousand workers walked out. That evening the shops were closed until further notice.

A few days later, the town of Pullman had another visitor, but one who had not come to admire its architecture or its landscaping.

Eugene Victor Debs, head of the newly organized American Railway Union, to which Pullman's workers belonged, had advised against the strike. But on May 16 he arrived to express his sympathy for the workers and deliver a caustic attack on George Pullman. "The paternalism of Pullman is the same as the self-interest of a slave-holder in his human chattels," he told the workers. "You are striking to avert slavery and degradation."

Tall, lean, with penetrating, deep-set eyes and thinning hair above a high forehead, Eugene V. Debs—at the age of thirty-nine—did not look like the sort of man who would lead a revolution. But before the Pullman strike was over, the labor upheaval that began there would be referred to as the Debs Rebellion.

Serious and absolutely dedicated to his union cause, Debs in his rumpled tweed suit might have been taken for a college professor. Generous to a fault and always convivial, he often was admired even by those who opposed him in labor disputes and was loved to the point of idolatry by his host of followers. "God was feelin' mighty good when he made Gene Debs," poet James Whitcomb Riley once said, "and He didn't have anything else to do all day."

The son of Alsatian immigrants, Debs had quit school and gone to work in the railroad yards of his hometown, Terre Haute, Indiana, when he was only fourteen. Four years later, in 1874, Gene joined the local lodge of the Brotherhood of Locomotive Firemen, and in 1880 he became national secretary-treasurer of the order and editor of its official magazine.

The BLF was one of several national railway brotherhoods that were more protective fraternal organizations than they were trade unions. They avoided strikes over wages and hours and concentrated instead on raising funds to pay accident and death benefits.

Gene Debs gave twelve years of his life to the brotherhood and largely succeeded in turning it into an effec-

A certificate of membership in the Brotherhood of Locomotive Engineers—representing workers from Canada to Mexico—carries symbols of such virtues as sobriety.

92

tive national organization. Yet the firemen, he came to realize, never could achieve their legitimate demands for a better life so long as they were not united with the locomotive engineers, the switchmen, the conductors, and the yardmen.

Beginning in 1889, Debs attempted to form a federation of the brotherhoods. Three years later, his efforts a failure, Debs quit his post in the BLF and started to recruit other railroad men dissatisfied with the complacent brotherhoods. On June 20, 1893, at Chicago, he launched the American Railway Union.

When he arrived at Pullman in May, 1894, Debs represented an organization of 150,000 men and he had just won an impressive victory in a strike against James Jerome Hill's Great Northern Railway.

At the ARU's national convention, held one month later in Chicago, the Pullman strikers presented an agonized appeal for support.

A thin young seamstress named Jennie Curtis rose to tell her bitter story. After working for the Pullman Palace Car Company for thirteen years, her father had died, leaving her a debt of $60 in back rent due the company. Since $14 of her monthly paycheck of $20 went for current rent at one of Pullman's model flats, it would be years before she could be debt-free.

"We ask you to come along with us," Jennie said to the delegates, "because we are not just fighting for ourselves, but for decent conditions for workers everywhere."

The seamstress' plea was irresistible, and the ARU voted to sup-

Contemporary press pictures, such as these, often exaggerated the violence of the Pullman boycott. Above, strikers overturn freight cars; at right, troops escort a train past strikers.

port the Pullman strikers. If the company failed to negotiate by June 26, other Pullman shops would be struck. More importantly, ARU members across the country would refuse to work trains to which Pullman sleeping cars were attached.

When the deadline passed without a word from Pullman, Gene Debs ordered Pullman cars cut from trains and sidetracked. The railroads immediately stopped most trains, arguing that their contracts prohibited them from running without sleeping cars. At the end of three days 125,000 men on twenty railroads had joined the boycott against Pullman cars.

The struggle initiated between the ARU and the railroads soon became a struggle between the union and the federal government in Washington. Within two days of the beginning of the boycott the Postmaster General was receiving reports from Illinois, Indiana, Idaho, and California that mail shipment was being hindered on the blockaded railroads. On July 1 Attorney General Richard Olney received even more alarming news: violence had broken out around Chicago.

Before entering President Grover Cleveland's cabinet, Olney had been a corporation lawyer serving as a director of several railroads. He was shocked now by the workers' audacity in stopping trains and immediately set out to break the strike.

On July 2 federal injunctions issued under the Sherman Anti-Trust Act of 1890 sought to halt the boycott. That same day the federal marshal at Chicago wired the Attorney General to say that local forces no longer could restrain the "rioting" strikers.

Federal troops, called out by President Cleveland in July, 1894, turned Chicago's Lake Michigan waterfront into a huge bivouac area. The troops were ordered to protect rail passage through the city.

Gene Debs, working almost round the clock since the beginning of the boycott, fell into an exhausted sleep in a Chicago hotel on the night of July 3. Early the next morning he was awakened by bugles outside his window and wondered sleepily if an Independence Day parade might be forming at that hour. When he peered out, however, he caught sight of hundreds of federal troops, encamped along Lake Michigan. Grover Cleveland had sent the Army to stop the strike.

"If it takes every dollar in the Treasury and every soldier in the United States Army to deliver a postal card in Chicago," Cleveland told a friend, "that postal card shall be delivered." The combined force of federal court injunctions and federal troops proved too much for the railroad strikers; within two weeks the Pullman boycott collapsed in complete defeat.

A few days before the end of the strike Debs and other officers of the ARU were arrested on a federal charge of conspiring to interfere with interstate commerce and the delivery of mail. Though never convicted on this count, Debs later served a six-month sentence in McHenry County jail at Woodstock, Illinois, for a lesser offense arising from the strike.

When Eugene Debs came out of the Woodstock jail, Sam Gompers wrote, "He had lost all faith in the power of constructive work and became the advocate of revolt."

The A.F. of L. chieftain's remarks reflected his antagonism toward socialism and the ARU, which he considered a potential rival to his own organization. Yet Gompers' accusation was not far from the mark.

During his months in jail Debs read or reread the classics of socialism and apparently became converted to its radical political program. Upon his release he attempted to revive the ARU but succeeded only in paying the dying organization's debts by extensive lecture tours around the country.

After the ARU finally expired in 1897, Debs helped found the Socialist Party of America and—though active for a time in the Industrial Workers of the World—he devoted the rest of his life to political affairs. Five times the

Socialist candidate for President, Debs achieved the distinction of polling nearly 1,000,000 votes in 1920 while serving time in a federal prison for opposition to U.S. participation in World War I.

At his death in October, 1926, Eugene V. Debs no longer was remembered primarily as a union leader. His role as a socialist and champion of many radical causes had taken him out of the mainstream of the American labor movement. Yet workers everywhere paused to mourn this gentle, thoughtful man who once had dreamed of uniting American railroad workers in one large union.

The burly man with a large round face under a shock of dark hair stood up and squinted through his one good

UPI

A resolute Eugene Debs appears (left) with his 1908 running mate on a campaign poster. In 1920 he ran for the presidency while serving a term in prison. At right, Debs is seen giving a fiery speech.

eye at the hundreds of upturned faces in the crowded hall. Perhaps the whispers and murmurs of the delegates and spectators seated out front angered him, for suddenly Big Bill Haywood stooped down, picked up a loose board from the platform to use as a gavel, and banged for order.

"Fellow workers . . ." he called. "This is the Continental Congress of the working class. We are here to confederate the workers of this country into a working-class movement that shall have for its purpose the emancipation of the working class from the slave bondage of capitalism. . . ."

Behind Haywood on the platform that day—June 27, 1905—sat Eugene Debs. In the audience were representatives of 140,000 workers: the Western Federation of Miners, to which

Haywood himself belonged; the United Brewery Workers, an industrywide union grown disillusioned with the narrow trade unionism of the A.F. of L.; the United Metal Workers; and the Socialist Trade and Labor Alliance, a left-wing group founded ten years earlier by a former Columbia University professor named Daniel De Leon.

This divergent group of labor leaders, reformers, and political agitators really had only two basic ideas in common: disillusionment with the existing order in the United States and disgust with such moderate labor leadership as that provided by Sam Gompers and the American Federation of Labor. Only a complete overhaul of the government could bring justice to American workers. As a

99

step in that direction, these delegates were to form the nation's most radical and most colorful labor organization, the Industrial Workers of the World.

The choice of Big Bill Haywood to open the first convention of the IWW was a most fitting one, for he—perhaps more than any other delegate there—symbolized the discontent and even despair of America's lower-class "working stiffs."

Born in Salt Lake City in 1869, Bill Haywood had lost an eye in a boyhood accident. Despite this handicap, he went to work in a Nevada mine at the age of fifteen.

Like many Westerners of his generation, Bill Haywood did not stick to one calling. In the next few years he tried his hand at bronco-busting on a ranch and at homesteading. When he lost his farm to the government, he went back to mining.

Haywood roamed the West—Nevada, Utah, Idaho—working wherever and whenever he could. In the summer of 1896 he was at Silver City, Idaho, recovering from a mine injury that almost had cost him a hand, when Edward Boyce, president of the three-year-old Western Federation of Miners, came to organize the region's miners. Haywood was an immediate convert, and within four years he was the organization's secretary-treasurer.

Boyce, Haywood, and their followers felt that western miners had little in common with the United Mine Workers who represented the coal miners of the eastern states. They built the Western Federation of Miners into a boisterous, aggressive organization that truly represented the rough-and-tumble spirit of the Old West. WFM strikes had led to violence and bloodshed, as mine owners' brutality all too often was met with assassination and dynamite. The biblical injunction "an eye for an eye; a tooth for a tooth" temporarily ruled the West.

Sam Gompers made an uneasy alliance with the WFM. But Haywood had little respect for the A.F. of L. chieftain, calling him a "squat specimen of humanity" with a "vain, conceited, petulant, and vindictive" personality.

Leaving the Federation, the western miners made two abortive efforts to form their own national organization, the Western Labor Union in

Feared and denounced as a radical, Bill Haywood looks like a respectable businessman in this photo of a relaxed moment.

1898 and the American Labor Union in 1902. Neither body succeeded in taking root and growing. Thus, by June, 1905, the Western Federation of Miners was eager to join other dissenters in launching the IWW.

Because the IWW was formed of so many different groups, its first few years were spent mostly in internal disputes, as its members squabbled among themselves about unionism, socialism, and anarchy. Not until 1908 did the IWW settle these arguments—and then only by secession and expulsion of dissenters. By that year, Debs and De Leon had left the IWW, and the Western Federation of Miners had withdrawn its support. There were perhaps only 6,000 members left, but this hard core shortly would build the IWW into a large and powerful group.

In the meantime, Big Bill Haywood was not thinking much about the IWW, for he was in deep trouble.

On December 30, 1905, former Governor Frank Steunenberg walked through the snow to the garden gate of his home at Caldwell, Idaho. As Steunenberg touched the gate, he triggered a bomb that fatally wounded him.

During his term of office that had ended four years earlier, Governor Steunenberg had dealt harshly with the WFM and had called out troops to break up strikes. Within a month of Steunenberg's assassination, a man named Harry Orchard had confessed to the crime and had implicated Haywood, Charles Moyer, new president of the WFM, and a Denver shopkeeper named George Pettibone.

Without a warrant and without extradition papers, Idaho authorities seized the three men at Denver on the night of February 17, 1906, and took them by private train to a Boise prison.

Although Idaho's seizure of the three men in Colorado was completely illegal, Haywood, Moyer, and Pettibone were kept imprisoned for over a year; not until May, 1907, did Haywood's trial for murder begin.

The Haywood case became a national labor crusade, and the famous Chicago lawyer Clarence Darrow was engaged to defend Big Bill. Darrow succeeded in winning a "not guilty" verdict for Haywood—and later Moyer and Pettibone also were exonerated. But during the course of the trial, Haywood broke with Moyer and with the WFM. After his release he devoted the rest of his career to the struggling IWW.

By this time, the IWW was turning to the disenchanted and disenfranchised everywhere—not only the miners of the West, but also the migratory farm workers of the Southwest, the lumberjacks of the Pacific Northwest, the cowboys of the plains, the immigrant factory workers of the East, and even the wandering, homeless hobos. "Hallelujah, I'm a bum!" became the theme song of these devoted believers in One Big Union, and the message was carried on stickers

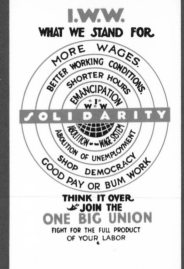

A montage of the posters that carried IWW slogans across the country is arranged about the masthead of Solidarity, *the Wobbly newspaper, in which the letters are composed of tools.*

pasted to boxcars that crisscrossed the country.

"We were indeed as sad a lot of unskilled, unorganized, overworked, and underpaid undesirables as could be imagined . . . ," an IWW organizer and editor later wrote. "Youth has a logic all its own, and the IWW was an organization of young men. Sometimes it pays to be out of step with the world as I was at that time; sometimes it doesn't. In step or out of step, in jail or out of jail, we had the satisfaction of feeling that we were on the side of right and justice and that it was the other fellow who was beyond the pale. . . . We were rebels—and proud of it."

Respectable citizens came to fear this growing, shadowy power in the United States, and the IWW sarcastically was said to stand for "I Won't Work." And the organization had a nickname: the Wobblies.

According to one story, the name Wobbly originated with a friendly Chinese restaurant owner on the west coast, who had pledged to feed IWW strikers free of charge. Whenever a hungry striker walked in, the Chinese —in trying to say, "Are you IWW?" —would come out with "All loo eye wobble wobble?" And Wobblies they became, a name adopted as a badge of honor.

Among the abuses that Haywood and other IWW leaders sought to correct was the fleecing of gullible lumberjacks by employment agencies. Lumbering was a seasonal occupa-

A 1919 cartoon linked the IWW with the Bolsheviks, who had just seized control of Russia. A smirking devil beams his approval and encouragement of the two, shown with the torch and bomb they were accused of using in their efforts to destroy civilization.

tion, and the men drifted from state to state looking for work. A so-called employment agent would charge the men a fee for directing them to a camp where hiring was under way. Often, however, the men either never would be hired at the camp or would be fired on some flimsy pretext within a day or two. The agent—of course, acting in collusion with the foreman—then could send new men to the camp and collect additional fees.

In late 1908 IWW agitators arrived at Spokane, Washington, to help put an end to this practice. When the city fathers outlawed IWW meetings in the street, the Wobblies immediately launched a "free speech" fight, arguing that it was their constitutional right to address workers at peaceful assemblies. A call went out for men everywhere to come and fill the jails of Spokane by being arrested for making streetcorner speeches.

Hundreds of men flocked to the Washington city, and on the first day of the demonstration for free speech 103 men in succession mounted a soapbox. Each had time only to say, "Friends and fellow workers . . ." before being yanked down by the police and hauled off to jail. The procedure exhausted the police before it did the demonstrators. One man confidently stepped up to be arrested and made the customary opening remark. But no one approached him and he found, to his horror, that he had nothing further to say to the expectant crowd. "Where are the cops?" the man stammered, in a flustered plea for arrest.

The Spokane free-speech fight was repeated in a number of other western cities, but the Wobblies' most notable success in the years before World War I was scored in a strike of textile workers at Lawrence, Massachusetts.

Only a few miles down the Merrimack River from Lowell, Lawrence by 1912 was a typically grim industrial city. The happy farm girls spinning and weaving in model plants had vanished two generations earlier. Their places had been taken by non-English-speaking workers from eastern and southern Europe.

At Lawrence the American melting pot still was boiling furiously. Some twenty-five nationalities were represented in the city. Organizing such a babel of peoples proved to be too much, even for the indomitable Wobblies. A textile workers' IWW local formed in 1906 managed to recruit only 300 of Lawrence's 30,000 laborers.

When workers opened their pay envelopes on January 11, 1912, they noticed a wage cut of 32 cents per week. A small amount, yet it was enough to buy ten loaves of bread. Shouting "Short pay! Short pay!" the enraged workers stormed through the plants and out into the streets. By the next day, a general strike had shut down every one of the factories in Lawrence.

The small IWW local had no idea how to organize such a massive walkout, and in desperation its members called for help. Within days, Wobbly organizers—including Bill Haywood—were on the scene.

The state militia was called out, and one officer reported that most of his men were from Harvard and "rather enjoyed going down there to have their fling at those people." A parade of 15,000 strikers was broken up by fire hoses on January 15, but the icy water only seemed to solidify the resolve of the workers.

A sea of workers carrying American flags as symbol of their Constitutional right to demon-strate peacefully confront a line of armed troops in this photograph of the Lawrence strike. Below, water from hoses used by authorities during the conflict forces strikers off a bridge.

A group of children being evacuated from strike-torn Lawrence use the occasion to make a plea in behalf of their parents' cause. Police brutality in seizing children at the railroad station aroused sympathy for the workers.

A Boston lawyer was outraged at the use of fire hoses. "The militia should have been instructed to shoot," he complained. "That is the way Napoleon did it." Finally, in one clash between strikers and police a woman picket was killed—but ironically, three IWW members were charged with her murder.

It was a harsh winter, and the strikers soon ran out of money. In a move that dramatized their plight, the Lawrence workers began sending their children to friends and relatives in other towns. When the police realized that this would prolong the strike, they swooped down on the train station one day and seized forty children bound for Philadelphia. When the parents tried to intervene, they were clubbed by the police.

This foolish act of police brutality was almost the last gasp of the mill owners and the authorities who supported them. On March 1, the manufacturers announced a wage increase. The Wobblies had won.

The Lawrence victory naturally brought new converts to the IWW, but strangely enough, the Wobblies were unable to maintain a steady membership. There were other strikes in other places, but often—whether they ended in victory or defeat—workers drifted away from the IWW when the excitement died down.

Typical of the IWW's free-spirited members was Joe Hill, an itinerant poet who roamed the West, working at odd jobs and composing some of the fiery songs for which the Wobblies were famous. Often set to familiar popular tunes of the day, Hill's songs expressed the despair and the hope of the downtrodden.

If the workers took a notion
They could stop all speeding trains
Every ship upon the ocean
They can tie with mighty chains.
Every wheel in the creation
Every mind and every mill;
Fleets and armies of the nation,
Will at their command stand still.

In January, 1914, Joe Hill was arrested suddenly in Salt Lake City and charged with the murder of a local grocer. Despite the fact that the evidence presented against him was far from convincing, Joe Hill was convicted and executed.

Wobblies everywhere bitterly protested Hill's execution as nothing more than a reprisal for his membership in the IWW. Just before facing the firing squad, Joe wired Bill Haywood: "Good-by, Bill. I die a true blue rebel. Don't waste time in mourning. Organize."

In August, 1917, the Wobblies gained a second martyr when organizer Frank Little—then leading a strike against the Anaconda Copper Company at Butte, Montana—was seized in his hotel room by masked men, dragged on a rope behind a car for several miles, and hung from a railroad bridge outside of town. A penciled note found on his body read: "First and last warning."

By this time, the United States was at war with Germany, and the IWW found itself engaged in a different kind of struggle. To the Wobbly leaders World War I was nothing more than another form of capitalistic exploitation of working men, of every country. The industrialists, they felt, would get rich, while the working class would be killed in the trenches.

Although the IWW hesitated to take a forthright stand against the war, some of its leaders advised resistance to the draft. To a nation gripped by war fever, this sounded like treason, and the government moved swiftly against the Wobblies.

On September 5, 1917, Department of Justice agents swooped down upon the Chicago headquarters of the IWW and upon local offices throughout the country. All records and files and even office equipment of the organization were seized, and warrants for the arrest of scores of officers and leaders were issued. Bill Haywood was among those caught in the dragnet.

The following August, after a lengthy trial, Haywood and 100 other Wobblies were convicted of conspiracy against the government, fined up to $30,000 each, and sentenced to prison for as long as twenty years.

Within a year Haywood and some of the others were out on $100,000 bail, as they appealed their convictions. During this interval of freedom,

Big Bill tried to rebuild the fractured IWW, but an event at Centralia, Washington, seemed to show that the movement was doomed.

On November 11, 1919, the first anniversary of World War I's armistice, an American Legion parade turned into an assault on the Centralia IWW hall. Inside the building, dressed in his army uniform, was a lumberjack named Wesley Everest. "I fought for democracy in France and I'm going to fight for it here," Everest shouted as the Legionnaires broke in. "The first man that comes in this hall, why, he's going to get it."

After emptying his rifle into the crowd, Everest turned and fled, but the mob caught up with him at a nearby river bank. He tried to surrender to proper authority, but instead he was seized and mauled before being thrown into jail. That night the mob returned to pull Everest out of jail and to torture and mutilate him horribly before hanging him from a bridge outside of town.

Dispirited but not defeated, Haywood continued to speak in behalf of the IWW, but by mid-1920, he was physically and emotionally exhausted. That fall the court of appeals upheld the Wobbly leaders' conviction, and Haywood faced another nineteen years in prison.

A momentous event of 1917 had been the overthrow of Russia's czarist regime and the rise to power of the Bolsheviks, or Communists. Since then, word had been reaching Amer-

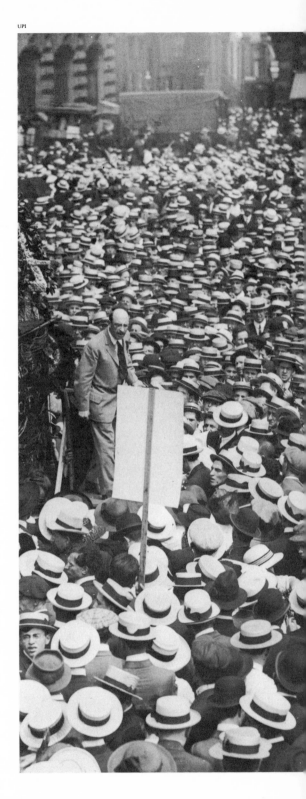

ica that Russia's new leaders were building a workers' paradise in that land, and Haywood secretly booked passage to the Soviet Union. Jumping bail to go to Russia, of course, meant that he never could return to America a free man.

Bill stayed below decks of the ship until it was out in New York Harbor and passing the Statue of Liberty. Saluting the statue, he said: "Goodby, you've had your back turned on me too long. I am now going to the land of freedom."

Unfortunately, Big Bill was to be sadly disillusioned. The Communists made a great deal of his defection from capitalistic America and tried to find some suitable position for him to fill in the Soviet Union. But he reportedly grew disillusioned with the "workers' paradise" and in his last years started drinking heavily. He died in Moscow on May 18, 1928, at the age of fifty-nine. Part of his ashes were buried in the Kremlin Wall, but part—at his request—were taken back to Chicago and placed next to the graves of the Haymarket martyrs.

A stormy figure in American history, Big Bill Haywood today is revered by some as a champion of the oppressed and denounced by others as a dangerous revolutionary.

Released from prison after serving 14 years for his attempt on Frick's life, Alexander Berkman (left) addresses a 1914 IWW rally in New York's Union Square. Berkman later was deported to Russia, home of self-exiled Bill Haywood, shown scowling above at the Kremlin.

6

A HOUSE DIVIDED

It was the last day of the 1935 A.F. of L. convention, held that October in Atlantic City, New Jersey, and a group of rubber workers had just submitted their application for an industrial union charter.

A giant figure rose from the carpenters' union delegation. The aptly named Big Bill Hutcheson—well over six feet tall, weighing upward of 300 pounds—had a point of order. "My point," he said, "is that the industrial union question has been previously settled by this convention."

William Green, president of the Federation since the death of Sam Gompers eleven years earlier, upheld Hutcheson's point. A few days before, the convention had voted overwhelmingly in favor of maintaining the A.F. of L. as an association of craft unions, such as that of the carpenters.

A minority of delegates on that occasion had argued for the establishment of industrial unions. In certain

"Think of me as a miner," John L. Lewis remarked late in his career as a controversial labor leader. At left, he visits a mine.

basic industries, such as steel, rubber, and automobiles, the type of work performed by a majority of workers did not really fall within the jurisdiction of any one particular craft. Rather, they said, all the workers in that industry, whatever tasks they performed, had a common interest that should be protected by a common union. Indeed, within the A.F. of L., there already were unions organized on an industrywide basis. Foremost among them was the United Mine Workers of America, headed by aggressive, irascible John L. Lewis.

Now Lewis stood to protest Green's ruling. "This thing of raising points of order all the time . . . is rather small potatoes," he said.

Bristling, the massive Hutcheson retorted: "I was raised on small potatoes. That is why I am so small."

Lewis, himself a bulky six-footer, had moved to the center of the floor. Now he turned to walk back to the mineworkers' delegation but paused en route next to Hutcheson.

"Pretty small stuff," Lewis snorted as he sized up the carpenters' chief. There was a further exchange, and the word "bastard" was heard distinctly in the hall.

In a flash, Lewis' right fist shot out and landed just below Hutcheson's eye. The two stout men—Hutcheson, 61 years old; Lewis, 55—grappled to the floor before their colleagues could separate them. Hutcheson, blood streaming from a cut on his face, was helped to the washroom, while Lewis walked away with only slightly injured dignity.

The dramatic fisticuffs at the 1935 convention only brought out into the open the simmering feud within the Federation between craft unionists and industrial unionists. It was the symbolic first blow in the civil war that was to divide and disrupt the house of labor for the next twenty years. And Lewis was to be the generalissimo of the industrial unionists for the initial campaigns of that war.

The eldest son of an immigrant Welsh coal miner, John Llewellyn Lewis had gone to work in the mines alongside his father in 1897, at the age of seventeen. Lewis' father once had been blacklisted for leading a strike, and the young miner took an early interest in unions. In 1906 he attended his first national convention of the United Mine Workers and apparently decided then to become a union leader.

Lewis' home—Lucas, Iowa—was too insignificant a locale from which to launch a national career in the labor movement, however, and shortly he moved to the larger coal-mining area of southern Illinois. Along with John went his five brothers, and the six Lewis boys soon had set up a family claque at union meetings. Within a year John was president of his new local.

When a mine accident killed 160 workers, Lewis almost physically coerced the state legislators into passing safety measures for the state's mines. In 1911 the A.F. of L. granted an industrial union charter to the United Mine Workers, and Sam Gompers singled out Lewis for assignment as an A.F. of L. field representative.

Yet Lewis remained faithful to the mineworkers, and in 1916 he became chief statistician of the union, with headquarters in Indianapolis. Four years later, he became president; just turned forty, Lewis was to hold the post for the next forty years.

In 1921 the ambitious Lewis attempted the impossible: he contested Sam Gompers for the presidency of the American Federation of Labor—an election he was foredoomed to lose. Lewis' fellow miner William Green made the nominating speech.

Unable to become king, Lewis contented himself with becoming kingmaker. When Gompers died in 1924, it was Lewis who engineered Green's election to the presidency of the A.F. of L. And for the eleven years leading up to the dramatic 1935 convention, Lewis supported Green.

Following the slugfest between Hutcheson and Lewis, the convention upheld Green's ruling in favor of Hutcheson. Another motion in favor of industrial unionism then was defeated by the delegates, and the convention proceeded to the election of officers as its final business.

His anger apparently abated, John L. Lewis rose—as he had in many years past—to nominate Green for reelection to the presidency. After his automatic endorsement by the delegates, Green made a graceful acceptance speech.

It had been an historic convention, Green remarked, perhaps the most historic in the Federation's history. Though torn by "conflicting emotions," the A.F. of L. had come through with "flying colors." It was time now to forget, he concluded. "The debate is over. The problems have been solved. A settlement has been made, and from this convention we must go out united."

William Green proved to be a poor prophet. The A.F. of L. in 1935 was, according to one historian, "stale and . . . overdue for renovation." Organized labor had not really shared in America's unprecedented prosperity of the 1920's. Indeed, in that decade, membership in the Federation had dropped from a 1920 peak of 4,000,-000 to 2,700,000 in 1929. When the stock market crash of 1929 precipitated the Great Depression of the 1930's, a weakened labor movement found itself powerless to help the millions of unemployed.

The standpatters of the labor movement, such as Green and Hutcheson, wanted to protect whatever they

WHICH WAY, LABOR

A 1936 newspaper cartoon graphically illustrated the split in the American labor movement. John L. Lewis and William Green pull an unhappy fellow in opposite directions.

had. In their view, the skilled workers of the Federation's craft unions should take care of themselves first—without concern for the unorganized and largely unskilled workers in the giant mass production industries. John L. Lewis vehemently opposed this "do-nothing" philosophy of the Federation's leaders.

As he surveyed the labor scene at the beginning of the 1930's, Lewis saw that unions in the auto, lumber, rubber, and cement industries had all but disappeared. There were no unions at all in meat packing, electrical manufacturing, aluminum, and the fledgling aircraft industry. The unions that existed in the oil, steel, textile, metal-mining, and brewery sectors were ineffectual.

Depressing, tumbledown houses were home to these offspring of Pennsylvania miners.

The only unions of any consequence, in fact, were Lewis' own mineworkers, those of the garment workers, building-trade organizations, such as the carpenters, and the railroad brotherhoods.

The strength of the United Mine Workers, on the eve of the historic 1935 convention, was due almost wholly to the singleminded persistence of John L. Lewis. Parallel to the decline of the A.F. of L. in the 1920's, Lewis' own union had weakened disastrously. At the end of the decade no industry was sicker than the coal industry. In a few distressed areas, un-

employed miners were operating closed and abandoned mines and selling the coal for whatever they could get. Yet through sheer force of personality, Lewis managed to hold his union together. His dictatorial conduct of national mineworkers' conventions was legend.

Many a UMW convention erupted into bedlam as opponents of Lewis' ironfisted regime physically stormed the rostrum he held like a fortress. "May the Chair state," he said to one unruly group of delegates, "that you may shout until you meet each other in hell and he will not change his ruling." One group of miners seceded to form a rival union, but Lewis' UMW continued to be the dominant organization in the industry. In 1933 he launched a mammoth organizing drive that brought membership up from 100,000 to an astounding 400,000.

Still Lewis was dissatisfied. The UMW had been unable to get even a toehold in the so-called captive mines —coal mines operated by the giant steel companies. And the steel industry, just as it had been in the days of Carnegie, was adamantly opposed to unions.

It was on this very point that Lewis had risen to address an early session of the Atlantic City A.F. of L. convention in October, 1935. The mineworkers, he argued, were anxious to have collective bargaining established in steel because only then would "the great captains of the steel industry" stop their efforts "to destroy and punish and harass our people who work in the captive coal mines . . .”

Lewis and his few but powerful allies in the Federation adopted a slogan: “Organize the unorganized.” As long as the legions of workers in the mass-production industries remained unorganized and outside the A.F. of L., they stoutly maintained, just so long would the Federation fail to be effective and truly representative of America's workers.

The morning after William Green gave his optimistic concluding address to the tumultuous convention, John L. Lewis sat down to a late Sunday breakfast in the dining room of Atlantic City's President Hotel. With the A.F. of L. convention adjourned, Lewis and his eight companions that day were setting out, in the words of one historian, “to adjourn the American Federation of Labor, permanently, if possible.”

Among Lewis' fellow “conspirators” were Philip Murray, vice-president of the UMW; Charles P. Howard of the International Typographical Union; David Dubinsky of the International Ladies Garment Workers Union; and Sidney Hillman of the Amalgamated Clothing Workers.

Lewis told the group of his plan to bring all of America's workers into a great new labor movement. His enthusiasm was contagious, and three weeks later, on November 9, the same group—with a few additions—met in Washington to form the Committee for Industrial Organization, or CIO.

When Green heard of the new group, he sent word to each member of the Committee of his “deep fears” that the CIO—although its members

Not a single smile brightens this conference of A.F. of L. and CIO leaders, held in March, 1939, at the request of President Roosevelt, who urged the labor groups to patch up their differences. The men at left represent the bricklayers, photo engravers, garment workers, and teamsters, all A.F. of L. unions. At right, the CIO's Sidney Hillman, Philip Murray, and Lewis.

Labor Day Amenities.

Another cartoon version of labor's split shows Lewis and Green taking their hefty "wives" for a Labor Day promenade and finding it difficult to restrain their "children" from an open fight.

still were in the A.F. of L.—might end up as a rival union, in opposition to the Federation. Lewis' tart reply was to resign his position as a member of the Federation's Executive Council. "I have neither the time nor the inclination," he said, "to follow the peregrinations of the Council from the Jersey beaches in the summer to the golden sands of Florida in the winter."

When the aroused Green threatened to excommunicate the CIO unions from the Federation, Lewis coolly retorted: "I fear his threats as much as I believe his promises."

As a former coal miner, William Green was still a member of the United Mine Workers and he nervously appeared before the UMW convention, early in 1936, to urge that his old union withdraw from the CIO. At the conclusion of Green's plea Lewis rose to ask how many of the 2,000 delegates agreed with the president of the A.F. of L. A single delegate rose, as 1,999 others hooted their disapproval. "There is your answer, Mr. Green," Lewis told his former comrade.

The breach widened through 1936, and at the November A.F. of L. convention, the ten CIO unions officially were suspended.

The mineworkers retaliated by dropping Green from their membership rolls, and temporarily, the head of the American Federation of Labor was a nonunion man. The sympathetic musicians' union remedied the situation by making Green a member. "That is appropriate," snapped Lewis. "Like Nero, Green fiddles, while Rome burns."

Meanwhile, the CIO already was proceeding with its ambitious program to organize the unorganized.

On January 19, 1936, thousands of Akron rubberworkers braved a blizzard to hear John L. Lewis call for a union at the Goodyear Tire and Rubber Company. Goodyear was among the giant firms maintaining "company unions" that were supposed to offer a partnership to employees.

"Partnership!" Lewis snorted. "Well, labor and capital may be partners in theory, but they are enemies in fact. . . ." Go to Goodyear, he suggested, and ask them for some of the stock dividends.

Ten days later, at another Akron rubberworks, Firestone Tire Plant No. 1, the night-shift foreman was nervously pacing the long ranks of his assembly-line workers. Despite freezing temperatures outside, the workers sweated at their mechanical chores. The clock's hand jumped to two.

At the end of the assembly line a tirebuilder glanced at the clock, gulped, and lifted his hands from his work. Down the lines other hands hesitated, hovering over the mechanical belt carrying the tires past them. The first worker bolted up, walked a few steps to the master safety switch, and swiftly pulled the large handle.

At an instant the machinery in the plant stopped, and the workers—

geared to synchronized movements on the assembly line—rose as one and stepped back from their seats.

"It's like the end of the world," one worker whispered in the unaccustomed silence. Then, as the Firestone tirebuilders realized what they had done, shouts of "We done it! We done it!" broke out. Firestone Tire Plant No. 1 was on strike—but this was a new kind of strike.

Rather than refuse to come to work and picket the company's plants, Firestone workers were staging the United States' first major "sit-down," a strike in which workers refused to vacate their factories until a settlement with management had been reached. It was a technique soon adopted in other major industries.

Among the leading targets of Lewis' campaign to organize the unorganized was the automotive industry. The giant corporations—Ford, Chrysler, and General Motors—had kept a tight lid on union organization in their huge plants. In one two-year period, 1934 to 1936, GM was reported to have spent more than $800,-000 for labor spies, men who would work in the factories and report on any union activities. Anyone even suspected of union membership would be summarily dismissed, and workers avoided talking to one another at lunch periods for fear that they would be accused of trying to organize. By 1936, the struggling young United Automobile Workers union had managed to organize only 20,000 out of

118

Strikers seeking recognition of the UAW in early 1937 used a dramatic new technique—the sit-down. Inside GM's Fisher body plant, workers lounge on car seats and play ticktacktoe on an auto trunk.

445,000 workers in the industry. It turned to the CIO for leadership.

In November and December spontaneous sit-down strikes were breaking out in automotive industry plants from Georgia to Michigan.

General Motors' executive vice-president William Knudsen agreed to "a personal interview" with Homer Martin, the UAW head. At the interview Knudsen informed Martin that GM would deal with its workers on a plant-by-plant basis and not with one union representing the industry.

Three days after Christmas, 1936, a new rash of sit-down strikes began breaking out in GM plants, with those in Michigan setting the pace. The siege was to last forty days.

To one cartoonist the sit-down was as unorthodox as a boxer pinning down his opponent in the ring merely by sitting on him.

Michigan Governor Frank Murphy arranged an armistice in mid-January, but just as the workers were marching out of the plants, it became known that GM was going to deal equally with the UAW and with its own company union, the Flint Alliance. The workers about-faced and resumed their sit-down.

At one point in the sit-down an overwrought Homer Martin was found wandering in the streets, tears streaming down his face, and he appeared ready to capitulate to General Motors. Someone should sit down on Martin, Lewis growled when he heard the story in Washington.

A bright young GM official next hit upon the idea of turning off heat in the plant, to force the workers out. This plan was quickly abandoned when it was realized that all the fire-fighting apparatus would freeze immediately, and with the apparatus out of order, the company's fire insurance policies would be invalid.

General Motors had obtained a court injunction calling for the evacuation of its plants by the sit-downers. But when it was discovered that the judge issuing the injunction was a major GM stockholder, the court order was ignored by the UAW with howls of laughter. Next GM forced Governor Murphy to call out the National Guard to protect its property. The possibility of bloodshed hovered over several Michigan towns.

"Unarmed as we are," the entrenched workers wired Governor

Murphy, "the introduction of the militia, sheriffs, or police with murderous weapons will mean a bloodbath. . . ."

In early February Lewis himself arrived on the scene, to bolster the wavering Martin and to take command of the strike in person. Told by Governor Murphy that the troops would have to be used to remove the sit-downers, Lewis coldly asked the Governor if he intended the Guard to used sharp-pointed bayonets that could be plunged in deeply or flat ones that could be twisted to make big holes.

With Lewis added to labor's negotiating team, the meetings between GM and the UAW became livelier if not immediately more productive. At one point Lewis politely asked one of the GM officials to move his chair a bit closer. When the executive protested that he already was within six inches of the CIO chief, Lewis purred that he merely wanted to tell his grandchildren that he once had sat only three inches away from one and one-half billion dollars.

In later negotiations with Chrysler, Lewis sat impassively through an anti-union tirade by a company executive. When the man concluded, another Chrysler official, K. T. Keller, asked Lewis if he had anything to contribute. The union leader rose and said:

"Yes, Mr. Keller, yes, I have. I am ninety-nine per cent of a mind to come around this table right now and with one fell swoop wipe that damn sneer off your face!"

Philip Murray talks to reporters about his plans to unionize the huge steel industry.

John L. Lewis' most impressive physical feature was a pair of shaggy eyebrows; the bristling brows made him instantly recognizable and were a favorite with cartoonists. In one later meeting with Chrysler, Lewis venomously denounced one of the corporation's executives. Exasperated beyond endurance, the man suddenly shouted: "Stop it, stop it, Mr. Lewis. I . . . I want you to know, Mr. Lewis, that I . . . I am not afraid of your eyebrows."

Such negotiating tactics as these, plus of course the persistence of the sit-downers, finally led to General Motors' capitulation. On February 11, 1937, GM recognized the UAW.

"It was like we was soldiers holding the fort," a striker later recalled of the historic sit-down. "It was like war. The guys with me became my buddies. I remember as a kid in school readin' about Davey Crockett and the last stand at the Alamo. You know, mister, that's just how I felt. Yes, sir, Chevy No. 4 was my Alamo."

Within a month of the pacesetting automotive settlement John L. Lewis and the CIO had achieved an even greater breakthrough.

From the days of Carnegie and Frick at Homestead the steel industry had steadily maintained its opposition to unions. The Amalgamated Association of Iron, Steel, and Tin Workers was a pathetic shadow by the mid-1930's; it represented less than 10,000 of America's 479,000 steelworkers.

On June 4, 1936, with the Amalgamated Association's approval, Lewis announced formation of the Steel Workers' Organizing Committee. This new group, headed by Philip Murray, would be responsible for a giant union drive in the steel industry.

Before the SWOC could make much progress, the spontaneous General Motors strike had broken out, and for a time all the CIO's energies were directed to that mighty contest.

In December, 1936, before he left for Michigan, John L. Lewis—according to one story—was dining one evening at Washington's fashionable Mayflower Hotel. Across the room sat Myron C. Taylor, chairman of the board of United States Steel, and Mrs. Taylor.

Mrs. Taylor, of course, recognized the famous labor leader, and on an impulse told her husband that she would like to be introduced to Lewis. Taylor already had been dealing with Lewis and obliged his wife by presenting her to the labor chieftain.

From this incident, apparently, stemmed a personal as well as a professional friendship between the two men. At frequent secret meetings in Washington and at Taylor's New York apartment the two men worked out an agreement by which U.S. Steel, on March 2, 1937, recognized the SWOC, later the United Steelworkers of America. Along with recognition, U.S. Steel raised minimum daily wages to $5 and granted a forty-hour week with time-and-one-half pay for overtime.

With such victories in his pocket, Lewis saw membership in the CIO soar. In the nine months ending with September, 1937, three million workers had voted for industrial unionism, and the CIO—the initials soon standing for the Congress of Industrial Organizations—claimed a membership of 3,718,000. It thus topped the A.F. of L., with 3,271,000 members, to become America's largest labor group.

John L. Lewis, in 1937, was a power in the land, and he knew it. A lifelong Republican, he was one of the few leaders of labor who had failed to support Franklin D. Roosevelt's first bid for the White House, in 1932.

One of Roosevelt's first New Deal measures had been the National Industrial Recovery Act. Section 7(a) of this law guaranteed labor's right "to organize and bargain collectively through representatives of their own choosing." In 1935 the Supreme Court declared the act unconstitutional, but the guarantee of collective bargaining was re-enacted almost immediately in the National Labor Relations Act, or Wagner Act. A National Labor Relations Board was set up to supervise plant elections in which workers could declare for or against a union. And certain employer practices, such as forming "company unions," were banned.

Impressed by this and other Democratic legislation favorable to workers, Lewis became an enthusiastic supporter of Roosevelt. In 1936 the CIO contributed $500,000 to Roosevelt's successful bid for re-election.

It soon was apparent that Lewis expected some return on his money, and he complained bitterly to friends that FDR failed to consult him often enough. In the summer of 1937 the CIO was engaged in yet another strike, this time with the smaller steel corporations. Asked for his opinion of the strike, Roosevelt flippantly answered by quoting Shakespeare's "A plague o' both your houses!"

Lewis, eyewitnesses reported, turned black with rage when he was

© 1948 *Esquire*

With his thick, bristling eyebrows and his shaggy mane of hair, portly John Llewellyn Lewis was the delight of all cartoonists.

"Team with Roosevelt" was an early FDR election slogan. At right, the candidate shakes a miner's hand during a campaign tour of West Virginia.

told of the President's remark, and from that moment he was consumed with implacable hatred for Roosevelt.

A month later, in a coast-to-coast radio address on Labor Day, September 3, 1937, Lewis denounced first the Roosevelt administration and then the President personally:

Labor, like Israel, has many sorrows [he dramatically intoned]. Its women weep for their fallen, and they lament for the future of the children of the race. It ill behooves one who has supped at labor's table and who has been sheltered in labor's house to curse with equal fervor and fine impartiality both labor and its adversaries when they become locked in deadly embrace.

As 1940 approached, there were strong signs that Roosevelt would break the two-term political tradition established by George Washington and seek a third term. Lewis sought an interview with the President and reportedly suggested himself for a spot on the 1940 Democratic ticket. "Which spot do you want," FDR is

supposed to have answered, "President or Vice-President?"

Lewis was not offered a place on the ticket and refused to endorse Roosevelt for a third term. Ten days before the election Lewis again went on nationwide radio to attack Roosevelt. After announcing his support for the Republican candidate, Wendell Willkie, Lewis offered a challenge: if FDR were re-elected, it would mean that organized labor had ignored Lewis' endorsement of Roosevelt's opponent. As a discredited labor leader, therefore, Lewis would retire promptly as president of the CIO.

Two weeks after the election, in which Roosevelt triumphed over Willkie, John L. Lewis kept his word. He resigned his leadership of the Congress of Industrial Organizations and saw his trusted lieutenant Philip Murray elected to replace him.

Yet the wars were not over for Lewis. He soon fell out with Phil Murray and had him ousted from the United Mine Workers—as he earlier had had William Green ousted. Lewis next took the UMW out of the CIO, applied for readmission to the A.F. of L., withdrew his application, and kept the mineworkers independent.

During World War II John L. Lewis earned even greater notoriety as he led his mineworkers in several strikes that threatened to halt wartime production.

"If a Gallup poll had been taken on the home front in May or June [of 1943]," a historian has written, "Lewis might have received a popular rating only a notch or two above that of Benedict Arnold."

Lewis justified his strikes with the complaint that whereas wages were frozen at a 1942 level, prices continued to soar. By and large, however, he did not feel—then or ever—that it was necessary to justify his actions. The coal miners, united in one of America's largest unions, were solidly behind him. "If John says the word," a miner was quoted as saying, "we'll all walk out. . . ."

After the war John L. Lewis continued to direct the mineworkers, maintaining his tight control until his eightieth year, in 1960. He took the UMW back into the A.F. of L. and back out again. He outlived his two bitter rivals, William Green and Philip Murray, and even saw the end of the division in the ranks of labor, with the 1955 merger of the A.F. of L. and the CIO.

John L. Lewis' stormy career as a national labor leader, stretching forty years, from 1920 to 1960, earned him many enemies. Dictatorial in running his own union, ruthless in his attempts to build a labor empire, cruel to old friends who disagreed with him, Lewis was unpopular with large segments of the American population.

Many people—reporters, politicians, industrialists, other labor leaders—tried to understand and explain John L. Lewis. He once offered his own simple clue: "Think of me as a coal miner, and you won't make any mistakes."

On a list of fifteen basic industries—such as steel, automobiles, printing, meat packing—the coal miners stood third from the bottom in weekly wages in 1939. Ten years later, after Lewis' many strikes, the coal miners topped the list, with a wage increase of 250 per cent. In addition, he had won portal-to-portal pay—for the dangerous travel underground—and health and welfare benefits for his miners. In 1946 he had won a $100-per-month pension for coal miners who had reached the age of 62 and had twenty years of service—the first such retirement plan achieved by a union in a major industry.

A national magazine, in 1949, set out to discover what rank-and-file union members thought of the controversial John L. Lewis. Reviewing the United Mine Workers' significant gains of the past four decades, an aged miner turned the question on the interviewer: "What do you think I think of John L. Lewis?"

. . . AND HE CALLED FOR HIS FIDDLERS THREE

TRUMAN, LEWIS AND CONGRESS FIDDLING

Copyright, 1950, by The Chicago Tribune

Postwar labor disputes in the coal industry inspired the above cartoon, in which John L. Lewis, President Truman, and Congress play a discordant tune for King Coal. Recurring strikes led to the restrictive Taft-Hartley Act, a measure bitterly resented by the labor unions.

126

7

A TIME OF TROUBLES

The President of the United States was furious. Through the spring of 1946 Harry S. Truman had been trying to head off a threatened strike against the nation's major railroads, but two of the twenty unions involved had refused to accept his compromise proposals.

In late May, Truman summoned to the White House the presidents of the hold-out unions: Alvanley Johnston of the Brotherhood of Locomotive Engineers and A. F. Whitney of the Brotherhood of Railway Trainmen. "You are not going to tie up the country," the angry Chief Executive told them. "If this is the way you want it, we'll stop you." The two men refused to accept Truman's final offer, however, and 300,000 workers struck on May 23.

Two days later, Truman went before Congress to denounce the "obstinate arrogance" of Johnston and Whitney, to call the walkout a strike against the government, and to ask for authority to draft into the Army all strikers so that he could keep the railroads running. As Truman was nearing the end of his impassioned address, he was handed a note: the strike had been settled, and on the President's own terms.

The brief railway strike that so greatly angered Truman was only one of many labor disputes in the year following the nation's victory in World War II.

During the war the federal government had been empowered to take over operation of any war industry threatened by a strike. But union leaders, including, most notably, John L. Lewis of the United Mine Workers, resented and sometimes even defied such controls.

With the war over, unions suddenly felt free to press the demands that they had been holding back during the conflict. Between November, 1945, and January, 1946, two million workers walked off their jobs, with strikes in such large industries as steel, automobiles, oil refining, meat packing, and electrical equipment manufacturing. Then came the railway strike and another walkout by Lewis' coal miners.

The public as well as Harry Truman grew angry. The strikes slowed

Senator Robert A. Taft (right) darts through a line of pickets protesting the Taft-Hartley Act. His sponsorship of the controversial law hurt his chances for a presidential nomination.

production at a time when there was unprecedented demand for automobiles, electrical appliances, and other consumer goods generally not available during the war years. Also, there was the fear that higher wages granted to strikers would lead to higher prices for these goods once they came on the market.

That fall the Republican Party captured control of both houses of Congress, and early in 1947 the GOP legislators set out to write a major new labor law.

Alarmed at the hostile attitude of Congress, the A.F. of L. appropriated nearly $1,000,000 to fight passage of what it later would term "a slave measure." President Truman, still basically sympathetic to the unions despite his anger of the year before, vetoed the legislation when it reached his desk. But in June, 1947, Congress overrode his veto to pass the Taft-Hartley Act.

The act reversed the trend of federal labor legislation, which had been generally favorable to the unions since the New Deal days of Franklin D. Roosevelt. The closed shop, one in which only union members could be employed, was outlawed. Jurisdictional strikes, to settle disputes between rival unions, and secondary boycotts—boycotts of firms doing business with companies whose employees were on strike—were banned. Court injunctions against strikes once more were to be permitted—thus the federal government could stop a strike for what was termed an "80-day cooling-off period."

Among the Taft-Hartley Act's more controversial provisions was one requiring union officers to sign an affidavit stating that they were not Communists. This struck at what many people considered a pressing problem of the postwar era: the infiltration of Communists into the labor movement.

During the late 1930's John L. Lewis had tolerated Communists in the swelling ranks of the CIO. "I do not turn . . . members upside down and shake them to see what kind of literature falls out of their pockets," Lewis said, brushing aside criticism.

During World War II, of course, the United States was allied with the Soviet Union against Hitler's Germany, and most members of the labor movement failed to see any peril in admitting Communists into the top ranks of union leadership. Only with the coming of the Cold War between the United States and Russia did the danger to the nation's economy of such infiltration become evident. The Communists, by then actually in control of some unions, seemed uncritically sympathetic to every Russian

move. Thus there was the possibility that strikes would be called, not to improve the workers' lot, but rather to weaken the United States at a time when the nation was confronting Soviet expansion.

One of the earliest fighters against Communism in unions was James B. Carey. Elected president of the CIO's United Electrical, Radio and Machine Workers Union in 1936 at the age of twenty-five, Carey was the nation's youngest union head in the prewar years. He was unaware, however, that some of his UE associates were Communists, and not until 1940 did he realize that he was being used by them to promote causes favorable to the Soviet Union. When he tried to break the Communist control of his union at the 1941 UE convention, he suddenly was ousted as president. Yet, James

James B. Carey (left) was denounced at the UE's 1948 convention because of his claim that Communists dominated the union.

Carey, who also was secretary-treasurer of the CIO, was not through with his fight.

In succeeding years Carey watched in anguish as the Communists penetrated other CIO affiliates, such as the National Maritime Union, the International Longshoremen's and Warehousemen's Union, and the Transport Workers Union—and even gained office in the national organization.

One of the leaders often accused of being a Communist was the garrulous Mike Quill, president of the Transport Workers Union. A CIO committee investigating Communist infiltration tried to pin down a witness on whether or not Quill had been a member of the Communist Party:

I couldn't prove a duck was a duck [the man testified], except it looks like a duck and the whole world says "That is a duck," and it quacks like a duck, and that is what I was taught, that it was a duck, and I was raised that way, so until my dying day, until they change a duck to another name, I am going to answer when people point at it that that is a duck.

Whatever his earlier affiliation, Quill at last broke with the Communists who had come to dominate his union. Appearing before a 1948 TWU meeting, he dramatically tore up an issue of the Communist newspaper, *The Daily Worker.* He would let neither his union nor the CIO be run "by a goulash of punks, pinks, and parasites."

Another defector from the ranks of Communist sympathizers—he al-

ways maintained that he never had been a Communist himself—was Joseph Curran, president of the National Maritime Union. When CIO president Philip Murray was alerted to the danger of Communism, the stage was set for a massive contest. The climax was reached at the 1949 CIO convention.

At the convention the anti-Communist forces were led by Walter Reuther, the articulate leader of the United Automobile Workers who recently had purged his union of left-wingers. In a ringing address to the delegates Reuther pointed out that there was room in the labor movement for an honest difference of opinion. What

Joe Curran seems undismayed by the threat splashed on his garage after he started to purge his union of pro-Communist elements.

130

Despite the attempts on their lives, Walter Reuther (right) and his brothers Roy and Victor (left) helped to reform their union.

there was not room for, he contended, was the "obstructionism and sabotage" carried on by the Communist minority.

The Communists, Reuther continued, were not trade unionists; they were not free men. "They are colonial agents using the trade union movement as a basis of operation in order to carry out the needs of the Soviet Foreign Office." He did not challenge the right of the Communists to proclaim their policies, Reuther stated. But he did challenge their right "to peddle the Communist Party line with a CIO label on the wrapper. . . ." That is what he, and the other reformers, were going to stop.

An indictment was drawn up against the United Electrical, Radio and Machine Workers, Carey's old union, and a resolution for the group's expulsion was presented to the convention. "We can no longer tolerate within the family of the CIO the Communist Party masquerading as a labor union . . ." By a resounding two-thirds vote, the UE was expelled.

In the following year other pro-Communist unions were driven, one by one, out of the CIO. In their place new groups were chartered. James B. Carey was named to head an independent electrical workers union, a group that soon outstripped the declining UE. In fact, of all the expelled unions, only Harry Bridges' International Longshoremen's and Warehousemen's Union, a Pacific Coast group, maintained its strength.

While the CIO was combating Communism, the rival American Federation of Labor was struggling with an equally serious problem—the infiltration of racketeers into its member unions.

Criminal elements began to worm their way into A.F. of L. affiliates in the 1930's. Not until the post-World War II years, however, did the extent of gangster control of unions become known—just about the time when people also were becoming aware of the Communist threat to the labor movement.

Perhaps the most notorious example of labor racketeering was uncovered in the powerful International Longshoremen's Association, a union that dominated Atlantic and Gulf

It took mounted police (upper right) to escort loyal ILA members to work on New York docks during the 1951 wildcat strike against union corruption. At left, strikers surge against a police cordon.

Coast docks. A 1951 wildcat strike by several New York locals first called attention to wide dissatisfaction with the leadership among rank-and-file members. And an investigation by the New York State Crime Commission soon brought to light the causes of this dissatisfaction.

The ILA, wrote *New York Times* reporter A. H. Raskin, had been transformed into "an amalgamation of gangs so powerful that the insurance companies and the police joined with the shipping lines and the stevedores in acknowledging and confirming their supremacy." The union, Raskin claimed, was "a Frankenstein monster" of the employers' own making. They kept the union president, Joseph P. Ryan, in cars and finery "right down to the pajamas he wore to bed at night," and they paid for "the hooligans Ryan recruited from Sing Sing to keep the rank and file in subjection."

Crime on the waterfront, wrote Malcolm Johnson, another New York reporter, had been "developed into a fine science involving false cargo receipts, checkers with phony pseudonyms, and watchmen who turn their backs at the right moment." One steamship line reported losses from organized theft at $3,000,000 annually, but few firms were willing to risk reprisals by complaining.

The union that was supposed to protect the workers instead fostered a primitive hiring method known as the shape-up. Men gathered on the docks each morning to be picked for that day's assignment by a union representative. Staying on the right side of the union and not protesting against any crooked dealings were essential if a stevedore wanted to maintain steady employment.

Another abuse was the so-called loading racket. Hoodlums on the docks would charge a fee to any trucker loading or unloading his cargo—even if the man did his own work. "If a truckman wants to do his own loading and unloading he can try it," wrote Johnson. "He had also better have a friend in the neighborhood to pick up the pieces."

The victimized stevedores found it dangerous to fight their corrupt union. A rank-and-filer who had led a wildcat strike against the ILA asked if he could come back to work after the protest collapsed. "Sure," was the reply, "but it will be your own fault if you fall and hurt yourself." Back on the job the rebel fell and hurt himself —in other words, he was beaten up. And that ended that rebellion.

The revelations about the ILA were so shocking that the leaders of the American Federation of Labor demanded an end to the corruption. After the Longshoremen failed to live up to promised reforms, the A.F. of L. voted overwhelmingly at its 1953 convention to expel the ILA. Efforts to launch a rival union met with failure, however, and the Federation learned that house-cleaning was a long and costly undertaking.

Communism and corruption, of course, are not the full story of the labor movement in the postwar years. But these issues seemed to grab the most newspaper headlines. Unfortunately, the activities of the large majority of union leaders—upright, faithful to their members, and loyal to the United States—often went unreported.

Sincere, scrupulously honest Walter Reuther lived modestly on his United Auto Workers' salary; any extra income from speeches and writings he turned over to a labor foundation. Offered an expense allowance of $50 per day, he said he could live well enough on the $12 that was standard for representatives of his union. Once an auditor found that Reuther had inadvertently charged the union for a $1.50 valet service; he promptly repaid the sum.

Ever zealous of his members' needs, Reuther in 1950 negotiated a five-year agreement with General Motors that set a postwar pattern and dramatically revealed organized labor's tremendous gains. Included in the package were such far-reaching items as a pension system, insurance benefits, and a cost-of-living adjustment that would increase wages in relation to rising prices.

Reuther did not rest on these hard-won gains. In succeeding years he championed a guaranteed annual wage to guard against seasonal unemployment; profit-sharing for the workers; and paid leaves-of-absence.

Reuther also was a leader in the movement to bring the nation's two giant labor organizations together again. Curiously enough, the postwar troubles—the CIO's principally with Communists and the A.F. of L.'s largely with racketeers—brought the rivals closer together. Both organizations strongly opposed the Taft-Hartley Act, and on a variety of other issues the once bitterly hostile groups often found themselves united.

On November 9, 1952, Philip Murray, president of the CIO for the previous twelve years, died of a heart attack. Less than two weeks later, William Green, president of the A.F. of L. for twenty-eight years, also died. With these two former coal miners—rivals for so many years—gone, it was possible to put aside the question of personal antagonisms and begin the search for a unified labor movement.

A merger of the A.F. of L. and the CIO became almost the first item of business for the two new presidents: George Meany, a former plumber and A.F. of L. secretary-treasurer since 1940, and Walter Reuther. Meany, Reuther, and their aides sat down on April 7, 1953, to discuss the situation.

The chief obstacle to unification, the two men realized, was "raiding," in which an A.F. of L. union would attempt to win members away from a similar CIO union, and vice versa. A study of the previous two years, however, revealed that out of these contests only 35,000 former CIO workers had been lured into the A.F. of L.,

Clasped hands against the outline of North America symbolized the merged AFL-CIO.

while some 27,000 A.F. of L. workers had been won over to the CIO. A net shift of 8,000 workers seemed hardly worth all the effort.

By June, 1953, Meany and Reuther had worked out a no-raiding agreement; within a year it was ratified by 65 of 110 A.F. of L. unions and 29 of the CIO's 32 unions. A constitution for the new group then was hammered out at a lengthy session in a Florida hotel—after which Meany sat down at a piano to serenade old friends and former enemies alike.

As the two organizations marched toward unification, someone asked Meany if the new labor organization would include John L. Lewis and his United Mine Workers. "Good Lord," exclaimed Meany, "he's the fellow that split the A.F. of L. He's the fellow who tried to split the CIO after he got tired of that. He's the fellow who came to the A.F. of L. in 1947 and tried to split it again." For the time being, John L. Lewis' United Mine Workers—along with the independent

At a 1951 meeting of union chiefs, David Dubinsky of the garment workers scores a point with George Meany (right) who succeeded William Green (center) as the head of the American Federation of Labor.

railway brotherhoods—would stay out of a merged labor union.

Finally, the two groups scheduled their 1955 conventions for the same time and place—the first week of December in New York City. They met only to adjourn and then at the 71st Regiment Armory, on Park Avenue at 34th Street, opened the first convention of the American Federation of Labor–Congress of Industrial Organizations—a group representing some 15,000,000 workers. After twenty years, America's house of labor was divided no more.

Labor's troubles, unfortunately, did not end with the merger. Only a year after those joyous unification ceremonies in New York, a young lawyer named Robert F. Kennedy was scurrying about the country gathering evidence of the misuse of funds by union leaders.

The corruption uncovered by Kennedy, a committee counsel for the U.S. Senate, proved to be so widespread that a special panel was formed in January, 1957, to explore the subject. The highly respected John L. McClellan, Democrat of Arkansas, was named chairman of this Senate Select Committee on Improper Activities in the Labor or Management Field. Among the first witnesses to appear before this so-called Rackets Committee was Dave Beck, president of the International Brotherhood of Teamsters.

The roly-poly little man—his round, pink face a wreath of smiles—beamed obligingly at the news photographers as he entered the hearing room in Washington's Capitol. Dave Beck—"His Majesty, the Wheel," as those who knew and respected his immense power called him—exuded confidence as he approached the front of the room and was seated at the small witness stand opposite the senators' long, smoothly polished committee table. Leader of the Teamsters for the previous five years, Beck was a first citizen of his home town, Seattle—Exalted Ruler of the local Elks Club and president of the Board of Regents of the University of Washington.

A few months earlier, Beck, a former laundry truck driver, had been received courteously at the White House by President Dwight D. Eisenhower, then seeking a second term. The Teamster boss had returned recently from Europe, where he had been greeted as one of America's outstanding "labor statesmen," and he now was being considered for presidential appointment as chief U.S. delegate to the United Nations' International Labor Organization.

The senators, Beck understood, were out to learn something about the workings of the American labor movement—and he was just the man to instruct them.

Across the table, seated next to Senator McClellan, was Robert F. Kennedy. Then only thirty-one, intense and boyish-looking at the outset

of his brilliant but tragically brief political career, Kennedy scrutinized the famous witness.

"I must confess," Kennedy later wrote, "that when Dave Beck first took the stand and before he started to testify, I felt sorry for him." In his files, Kennedy knew, was sensational evidence documenting Beck's misuse of union funds. The public figure now before the committee, so proud and self-assured, was "about to be utterly and completely destroyed before our eyes."

Through the morning and much of the afternoon Beck testified. His long, rambling answers to the senators' questions developed into lectures in which the portly labor chieftain aired his views on a wide range of topics. As leader of the nation's largest union—a fact that Beck repeatedly called to the attention of the senators—he favored legislation that would enforce strict accounting of union funds and provide for preservation of all union records.

Robert Kennedy was hard put to conceal his annoyance at Beck's bland and misleading replies to the committee's inquiries. Finally, toward the end of the day's hearings, Senator McClellan turned to Kennedy and graciously asked the young lawyer if he had any questions. Indeed, he had, Kennedy indicated.

In the next few minutes Kennedy asked a series of devastating questions to which he already knew the answers. Had Beck used union funds to build his $162,000 mansion in Seattle? Had the Teamsters' president used $85,000 of union money to buy such items as silk shirts, a radio, golf clubs, football tickets, nylon stockings, outboard motors, a twenty-foot deepfreeze, rugs, a love seat?—the list seemed interminable.

To these and to most other questions that Kennedy and the committee members asked Beck that day—and on succeeding appearances before the committee—the stout labor leader refused to answer.

The phrase "I must decline to answer on the grounds that it would incriminate me" became Beck's refrain. Under the Fifth Amendment of the U.S. Constitution, a person is protected from testifying against himself, and Beck—and many other witnesses before the Senate committee—invoked this protection in avoiding

His hand covering the microphone, Dave Beck (right) consults his attorney, Edward B. Williams, before replying to questions at the Senate hearing on his union affairs.

answers to embarrassing or incriminating questions.

Despite Beck's repeated denials, evidence continued to build up against him. On May 26, 1957, the disgraced unionist announced that he would not seek re-election to the Teamsters' presidency. At the end of the year a Washington state jury found Beck guilty of stealing union funds, and fourteen months later, in February, 1959, the ex-labor boss was convicted of income tax evasion. After the failure of all appeals, Dave Beck entered MacNeil Island Federal Penitentiary in Puget Sound on June 20, 1962, to begin serving a five-year sentence.

Robert Kennedy did not have long to rejoice over his work in exposing Dave Beck. In forcing Beck's retirement from the Teamsters' presidency, he inadvertently had paved the way to power for an even more dubious personality—James Riddle Hoffa.

Hoffa, at the time of Beck's disgrace, was nominally only ninth vice-president of the International Brotherhood of Teamsters. In reality, he was heir-apparent to the country's largest labor kingdom.

Born in Indiana in 1913, Jimmy Hoffa had the bleak childhood and youth typical of many labor leaders. His father, a miner, died of coal poisoning when Jimmy was only seven; the widowed mother moved her brood of four to Detroit, and there—quitting school after the seventh grade—young Hoffa went to work in a warehouse. One evening in 1932 Hoffa was unloading strawberries for a grocery chain when he hit upon a simple but effective method of remedying the grievances that he and the other laborers had against their employer. They simply refused to move the perishable produce into the warehouse. Within an hour management had capitulated to Hoffa's demands.

The successful young strike leader organized his fellow workers into a union and joined the Teamsters. At nineteen Jimmy Hoffa had put in his last day of physical labor and had become a full-time union leader.

In 1932 the Teamsters were one of the oldest but far from the largest of American unions. The group had been organized three decades earlier as an association of teamsters, drivers of horse-pulled vehicles. Hoffa was among those bright young leaders who was to see the brotherhood grow into the largest union in the nation—1,400,000 members in 1957—a group that came to control nearly everything that moved on wheels.

It is a Teamster who drives the mother to the hospital at birth [noted Robert Kennedy]. It is the Teamster who drives the hearse at death. And between birth and burial, the Teamsters drive the trucks that clothe and feed us and provide the vital necessities of life. They control the pick-up and deliveries of milk, frozen meat, fresh fruit, department store merchandise, newspapers, railroad express, air freight, and of cargo to and from the sea docks.

Organizing such an empire was not a weakling's job, and Jimmy

Hoffa was proud of his toughness. A stocky 180 pounds, only five feet, five and one-half inches tall, Hoffa could command respect and fear with the slightest frown on his pock-marked face.

Called upon to testify before the McClellan panel, he, like Beck, thought that he had nothing to fear. Hoffa did not know the depth of Robert Kennedy's passion to expose corruption in the unions.

Unlike Beck, however, Hoffa declined to hide behind the Fifth Amendment; early that year, the AFL-CIO executive council had stated that union officials invoking the Fifth Amendment to cover up wrongdoing had no right to hold office. Hoffa was not going to risk his position, and instead he relied upon what he claimed to be a poor memory.

"I am saying," he explained one day to McClellan during the hearings, "that to the best of my recollection I have no disremembrance of discussing . . . any such question." Hoffa, a disgusted senator complained, had the country's "most convenient forgettery."

Outside the committee room Hoffa appeared to be less careful—and very nearly ruined his career at its peak, as he was about to succeed Beck in the Teamsters' presidency.

Early in 1957 a lawyer and former secret service officer named John Cye Cheasty came to Robert Kennedy with a story that Hoffa had offered him $2,000 per month to spy on the committee. Kennedy believed Cheasty's story, took him on the committee staff, and gave him documents to pass on to Hoffa.

At 11 P.M. on March 13, as he was stepping into the elevator of Washington's Dupont Plaza Hotel, Hoffa was placed under arrest by FBI agents. Tailing Cheasty, they claimed to have seen him hand over Senate documents to Hoffa. The FBI also had pictures purporting to show Hoffa giving Cheasty money for the documents, and the government papers were still in Hoffa's possession.

To Kennedy this was an airtight case against Hoffa; if the cocky Teamster leader were not convicted, the committee counsel said, he would jump off the Capitol. But Hoffa had the country's most clever criminal lawyers—in the next few years the Teamsters would pay in excess of $700,000 for Jimmy's legal fees.

In July the jury in Hoffa's bribery case reached a verdict: not guilty. Hoffa's defense lawyer dryly offered to send Robert Kennedy a parachute for his promised jump.

The evidence against Dave Beck had revealed that the Seattle labor leader had misappropriated hundreds of thousands of dollars of union funds for his own use. In comparison with the evidence introduced against James Hoffa, this seemed like petty thievery.

From his Detroit local Hoffa had built his power steadily until he controlled the huge Central States Drivers Council, the first interstate organi-

The above picture allegedly showing Cheasty handing government documents to James Hoffa (right) was used by the government in its attempt to convict Hoffa of bribery. Right, Robert Kennedy uses a chart to show the network of services controlled by the powerful teamsters union in New York.

zation of long-distance truck drivers. He muscled his way into New York by setting up paper locals, nonexistent groups that nevertheless gave him voting strength in national Teamsters' meetings. To extend his power, Hoffa had not hesitated to consort with convicted criminals.

Hoffa and one of his Detroit sidekicks even had gone into the trucking

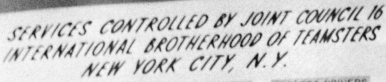

business—thus becoming employers as well as employees' representatives. To hide their involvement, a dummy corporation was set up, with Mrs. Hoffa and the other man's wife listed as owners of the firm.

Hoffa was accused of illegally transferring $500,000 of union funds to a Florida bank, in return for the financing of a land development scheme that he was backing. Sun Valley, Florida, was to be a retirement community for teamsters. When the scheme collapsed, some of the investors lost their precious lifetime savings, but not even this apparent betrayal shook the Teamsters' confidence in their Jimmy.

People outside the brotherhood were mystified by Hoffa's seemingly unshakable hold over his men. While Robert Kennedy was charging that Hoffa had sold out the union, a team of historians from California made an in-depth study of the Teamsters. No one knew the truck-freight industry better than Hoffa, they concluded, and no one was a tougher or more skillful bargainer for Teamsters' demands. Because of Jimmy, members of the giant union had higher wages, longer vacations, and better pensions than workers in most other industries. So despite the charges against him, the Teamsters remained loyal to Hoffa.

Perhaps most controversial of Hoffa's actions was his management of the Teamsters' Central and Southern States Pension Fund, worth some $300,000,000. Even the sympathetic California historians described Hoffa and the other trustees of the fund as a "group of overgrown adolescents playing 'Monopoly' but forgetting that this time the money and property are real."

With Hoffa's approval, money from the pension fund often was invested in unsound real estate projects that not only failed to return interest on the money lent, but sometimes even lost the principal as well.

As these charges against Hoffa gradually but relentlessly were introduced at the McClellan committee hearings, leaders of the AFL-CIO grew alarmed over the fate of its largest member union. The word went out that the parent body would expel the Teamsters should the union select Hoffa as Beck's replacement.

To no one's surprise, however, James Riddle Hoffa was elected to succeed Beck by a nearly three-to-one vote of the Teamsters' convention in October, 1957. Hoisting Jimmy to their shoulders, the joyous delegates marched, cheering, around the hall.

When the cheering stopped, however, Hoffa found that his troubles were far from over. A group of thirteen rank-and-filers took legal action to block Hoffa's assumption of the office, and on October 14 a federal judge issued a court order temporarily barring him from the presidency. Ten days later the AFL-CIO suspended the Teamsters from the Federation; in December the brotherhood finally was expelled.

Eventually, Hoffa gained his office —at first under the supervision of court-appointed monitors, but at last on his own. At a special Teamsters' convention in July, 1961, he was elected to a full five-year term at an annual salary of $75,000.

In the meantime, Hoffa had been tried and acquitted in other cases growing out of the McClellan investigation. But Robert Kennedy refused to give up.

Early in 1960 Kennedy resigned his Senate committee post to conduct his brother's successful campaign for the Presidency that year. And when John F. Kennedy took office as thirty-fifth President, Robert F. Kennedy became Attorney General.

A special "Hoffa unit" was set up in the Department of Justice, sixteen men who would devote nearly full time to finding evidence to convict Hoffa. It took the unit three years, but at last it was successful.

In December, 1962, a Nashville, Tennessee, jury failed to reach a verdict in a case growing out of Hoffa's privately owned trucking firm. The hung jury saved the Teamsters' boss from a one-year sentence on a misdemeanor. But as a result of this trial, Hoffa soon was charged with a felony carrying a longer term: jury tampering.

On the evidence of an informer within the brotherhood it was possible for the government to prove that Hoffa had attempted to bribe members of the jury in his Nashville trial. On March 4, 1964, a federal judge fined Hoffa $10,000 and sentenced him to eight years in prison.

The following month Hoffa entered another federal court, in Chicago, to face a twenty-eight-count indictment for fraud in handling Teamster money.

"I submit to you," the prosecuting attorney declaimed, "that [Hoffa and his codefendants] make Jesse James and his gang look like purse snatchers." The jury apparently agreed, and on August 17, 1964, Hoffa was found guilty on one charge of conspiracy and on three of fraud. He was fined $10,000 and sentenced to five more years in prison.

Hoffa naturally appealed his convictions, but time finally ran out for him in March, 1967. The U.S. Supreme Court refused to rehear his appeal, and the president of the nation's largest union entered a federal penitentiary, to begin serving the first of his two prison sentences.

The cases of Dave Beck and Jimmy Hoffa, unfortunately, were not unique. As a result of the McClellan investigation and of other probes, more union leaders were charged, tried, and often convicted of various crimes.

George Meany was among those most horrified by the revelations. The leaders of the Federation, he claimed, did not know "one hundredth" of the evidence of such corruption.

We didn't know that we had top trade union leaders who made it a practice to

His raincoat folded to hide the handcuffs he wears, an obviously embittered Jimmy Hoffa waits in the rain as a guard checks him through the gates of the federal penitentiary he entered on March 7, 1967. In 1968, when the Detroit teamsters local Hoffa still headed from prison held an election, a man who challenged Hoffa's rule was attacked (right) by a still-loyal follower.

secretly borrow the funds of their union [he protested]. We didn't know that there were top trade union leaders who used the funds for phony real estate deals in which the victims of their fraud were their own members. And we didn't know that there were trade union leaders who charged to the union treasury such items as speedboats, perfume, silk stockings, brassieres, color TV, refrigerators and everything else under the sun.

In the post-World War II era, however, American unions had other problems equally as important as fighting Communism and crime within their ranks. Chief among them, perhaps, was automation.

In the nineteenth century the first Industrial Revolution had transformed the United States from an agricultural to a manufacturing economy. After World War I the nation had entered another era in which mass production and the assembly line dominated its industries. Finally, after World War II, Americans experienced what some people were calling a second Industrial Revolution: the substitution of machines run by other machines for machines operated by men. This phenomenon of automation threatened to throw millions of workers out of their jobs.

In 1963 Walter Reuther noted that 68,000 jobs had been eliminated in the auto industry during the previous fifteen years—even at a time when production was being increased by three million units annually.

A century and a half earlier, men had expressed alarm over the arrival of the machine age. But as it turned out, more rather than fewer jobs were created by the first Industrial Revolution. The problem with automation, however, was the speed with which it was being introduced: there did not seem to be time in which unskilled or semiskilled workers could be trained for the more difficult task that they would be undertaking in the new era.

"There is no longer any question in my mind as to the direction in which automation is going today," George Meany told the 1963 AFL-CIO convention. "There is no element of blessing in it. It is rapidly becoming a real curse to this society." Meany also knew that in the future there were going to be fewer laborers, or blue-collar workers—the backbone of the labor movement—and more white-collar workers. And it was this group —clerical and sales personnel; professionals, such as teachers; and government employees—that the AFL-CIO largely had failed to organize.

At the 1955 merger a membership goal of double the 15,000,000 then represented was set for the next decade. Instead, the Federation in 1964— after the expulsion of the Teamsters and other corrupt unions—stood approximately where it had stood ten years earlier. And early in 1968 the labor movement again was split by a feud. Walter Reuther refused to pay the UAW's dues to the AFL-CIO and saw his giant union suspended from the Federation. A few months later, he formed a new grouping with the expelled Teamsters, the Alliance for Labor Action.

With only 18,000,000 Americans in all labor unions—out of a total work force of 75,000,000—organized labor still was no match for some of the nation's giant corporations. Nevertheless, the troubles of the postwar decades had turned many Americans against the labor movement—ironically just at the time when the unions were helping so many workers to achieve the equality and respectability that so long had been their goal.

Many of those who built the labor movement—at such a personal sacrifice—would have been greatly saddened to see the state of the unions in

the 1960's. This had not been the goal of Homestead workers facing the Pinkertons, of the cotton girls of Lowell singing during their "turnout," of William Sylvis dying in poverty, of Sam Gompers asking for "More."

What the workers and leaders of the past would have been proud of were the tremendous economic gains made by the laboring class in the century from 1860 to 1960. It was the unions, after all, that fought for the eight-hour day and the forty-hour week, for decent minimum wages in line with the cost of living, for vacations and holidays with pay, for medical benefits and retirement plans. And the gains that the unions won generally were passed on to those millions of unorganized workers, so that all Americans benefited.

The corruption of the few should not be allowed to obscure the accomplishments of the many; the "Reds" and racketeers should not overshadow the reformers. If the scandals and setbacks of recent years showed how far the unions of the United States still had to go, a brief look into the past will demonstrate even more clearly how far they have come.

In the age of automation such plants as Ford's Cleveland engine works (left) are dominated by machinery, with scarcely a worker in sight. Above, a solitary foreman controls an operation in a giant steel mill.

147

AMERICAN HERITAGE
JUNIOR LIBRARY

KENNETH W. LEISH, *Editor*

Janet Czarnetzki, *Art Director*

Sandra L. Russell, *Copy Editor*

Laurie P. Phillips, *Picture Editor*

Gay Sherry, *Text Researcher*

Annette Jarman, *Editorial Assistant*

ACKNOWLEDGMENTS

The Editors would like to thank the following individuals and organizations for their valuable assistance:

AFL-CIO, Washington, D.C.—Saul Miller
Los Angeles County Museum of Natural History—Mrs. Carol Arnold
The Metropolitan Museum of Art—Harriet Cooper
Ira Spanierman Galleries, New York—Mrs. Kathleen Hadfield
Tamiment Institute, New York—Dorothy Swanson

The Editors also would like to acknowledge the following sources: The quotations in Chapter 1 are from *Lockout, the Story of the Homestead Strike of 1892,* by Leon Wolff, published by Harper & Row, 1965. The quotations in Chapter 2 are from *The Labor Movement in the United States, 1860–1895,* by Norman J. Ware, published by D. Appleton & Co., 1929. The quotations on pages 49, 52, and 55 are from *The Path I Trod,* by Terence V. Powderly, published by Columbia University Press, 1940. The quotations on pages 56, 57, 58, and 59–60 are from *The History of the Haymarket Affair,* ©1936, 1964 by Henry David, published by Holt, Rinehart and Winston, Inc. The quotations in Chapter 4 are from *Seventy Years of Life and Labor,* by Samuel Gompers, published by E. P. Dutton & Co., Inc., 1925. The quotation on page 130 is from *The Communist Party and the CIO,* by Max Kampelman, published by Frederick A. Praeger, Inc., 1957. The quotations on pages 133 and 134 are from *Crime on the Labor Front,* by Malcolm Johnson, ©1950, used with permission of McGraw-Hill Book Company. The quotations on pages 137 and 139 are from *The Enemy Within,* by Robert F. Kennedy, published by Harper & Row, 1960.

FURTHER READING

The complete history of the American labor movement can be found in the following works:

Commons, John R., and associates, *History of Labour in the United States*, 4 vols. Kelley, 1918–35.
Dulles, Foster Rhea, *Labor in America*. Thomas Y. Crowell, 1960.*
Rayback, Joseph G., *A History of American Labor*. Free Press, 1959, 1966.*
Taft, Philip, *Organized Labor in American History*. Harper, 1960.

More information on the specific topics covered in this volume can be found in these books:

Adamic, Louis, *Dynamite, The Story of Class Violence in America*. Harper, 1931.
Alinsky, Saul, *John L. Lewis, An Unauthorized Biography*. Putnam, 1949.
Bernstein, Irving, *The Lean Years, A History of the American Worker, 1920–33*. Houghton Mifflin, 1960.*
Buchanan, Joseph R., *The Story of a Labor Agitator*. Outlook, 1903.
Brody, David, *Labor in Crisis, The Steel Strike of 1919*. Lippincott, 1965.*
Chaplin, Ralph, *Wobbly, The Rough-and-Tumble Story of an American Radical*. University of Chicago Press, 1948.
Cornell, Robert J., *The Anthracite Coal Strike*. Catholic University of America Press, 1957.
David, Henry, *History of the Haymarket Affair*. Farrar & Rinehart, 1936.*
Foster, William Z., *The Great Steel Strike and Its Lessons*. Huebsch, 1920.

Workers in New York's garment industry parade to gain new members for their union.

Ginger, Ray, *The Bending Cross, A Biography of Eugene Victor Debs.* Rutgers University Press, 1949.*

Gluck, Elsie, *John Mitchell, Miner.* John Day, 1929.

Goldberg, Arthur, *AFL-CIO, Labor United.* McGraw-Hill, 1956.

Gompers, Samuel, *Seventy Years of Life and Labor,* 2 vols. Dutton, 1925.

Grossman, Jonathan, *William Sylvis, Pioneer of American Labor.* Columbia University Press, 1945.

Harrington, Michael, and Jacobs, Paul, *Labor in a Free Society.* University of California Press, 1959.

Haywood, William D., *Bill Haywood's Book.* International, 1929.*

Howe, Irving, and Widick, B. J., *The UAW and Walter Reuther.* Random House, 1949.

Jacobs, Paul, *The State of the Unions.* Atheneum, 1963.

James, Ralph C., and James, Estelle D., *Hoffa and the Teamsters, A Study in Union Power.* Van Nostrand, 1965.*

Johnson, Malcolm, *Crime on the Labor Front.* McGraw-Hill, 1950.

Josephson, Hannah, *The Golden Threads, New England's Mill Girls and Magnates.* Duell, Sloan and Pearce, 1949.

Kennedy, Robert F., *The Enemy Within.* Harper, 1960.*

Kornbluh, Joyce L., ed., *Rebel Voices, An I.W.W. Anthology.* University of Michigan Press, 1964.*

Lens, Sidney, *The Crisis of American Labor.* Sagamore, 1959.*

Lindsey, Almont, *The Pullman Strike.* University of Chicago Press, 1942.*

Mandel, Bernard, *Samuel Gompers, A Biography.* Antioch Press, 1963.

McClellan, John L., *Crime Without Punishment.* Duell, Sloan and Pearce, 1962.

Mollenhoff, Clark R., *Tentacles of Power, The Story of Jimmy Hoffa.* World, 1965.

Powderly, Terence V., *The Path I Trod.* Columbia University Press, 1940.

Renshaw, Patrick, *The Wobblies, The Story of Syndicalism in America.* Doubleday, 1967.*

Sulzberger, C. L., *Sit Down with John L. Lewis.* Random House, 1938.

Taft, Philip, *The A.F. of L. in the Time of Gompers.* Harper, 1957.

————, *The A.F. of L. from the Death of Gompers to the Merger.* Harper, 1959.

Tyler, Gus, *The Labor Revolution, Trade Unions in a New America.* Viking, 1967.

Ware, Norman J., *The Industrial Worker, 1840–60.* Peter Smith, 1959.*

Wechsler, James A., *Labor Baron, A Portrait of John L. Lewis.* Morrow, 1944.

Weisberger, Bernard A., *Samuel Gompers.* Silver Burdett, 1967.

Widick, B. J., *Labor Today, The Triumphs and Failures of Unionism in the United States.* Houghton Mifflin, 1964.

Wolff, Leon, *Lockout, The Story of the Homestead Strike of 1892.* Harper, 1965.

*Also available in paperback.

149

Workers turn out farm machinery at Cyrus McCormick's factory in the 1880's.

INDEX

Boldface indicates pages on which maps or illustrations appear

A

AFL-CIO, formation of, 135, **135**, 136, **back cover**
and crime in unions, 142–143
membership of (*1955–1964*), 145
and problem of automation, 145
A.F. of L., *see* American Federation of Labor
Akron, Ohio, rubber industry of, 117–118
Altgeld, John P., Governor, 61
in cartoon, **88**, 89
American Federation of Labor, 84, 99, 100, 128
founding and organization of, 56, 67, 73, 75, 79, 87
growth of membership of, 73–76, 85–86, 87, 122
decline in membership of (*1920–1935*), 113, 114
difficulties of, 80–82
political orientation of, 82–83
and craft unionism, 111, 115
and formation of CIO, 115, **115**, 117
cartoon of, **116**
and crime in unions, 131, 133–134, 135

merger with CIO, 125, 135, 136
conventions of, 83, 111–115 *passim*
American Federationist, 80
American Labor Union, 101
American Railway Union, 98
formation of, 92, 94
and Pullman strike, 94–95, 97
Anaconda Copper Company, 107
Anarchism, 68–69
Apprenticeship, rules for, 37
Army, U.S., in Pullman strike, 96, **96–97**, 97
Assembly line, 145
Atlantic Monthly, quoted, 38
Automation, problem of, 145
age of, **146–147**, 147
Automotive industry, unionization of, 118, 120–121
sit-down strikes in, **118–119**, 120
cartoon of, **120**

B

Baer, George, Jr., quoted, 79
Baltimore, Md., railroad strike in (*1877*), 47

Beck, David, **138**, 139, 142
quoted, 138
investigation of, 136–138, 140
conviction and jailing of, 138
Berkman, Alexander, 20, **20**, 109, **109**
Bessemer converter, **22–23**, 23
Boston, Mass., development of Knights of Labor in, 47
Boston Manufacturing Company, 26
Boyce, Edward, 100
Boycott, 80
secondary, 129
Brewery Workers, United, 99
Bridge and Structural Iron Workers Union, International, 81
Bridges, Harry, 131
Buchanan, Joseph R., **44**, 53, 64
and Knights of Labor, 52–53, 61, 64
Buck's Stove and Range Company, 80

C

California, labor legislation of, 34, 41
Carey, James B., 129, **129**, 131
and Communism in unions, 129–130
Carnegie, Andrew, 15, 17, 84, 122

quoted, 17, 19, 21, 22
cartoon of, 18, **18**
and Homestead strike, 19, 22
Carnegie Steel Company, 11, 12, 15, 16, 18, 19, 20, 21
see also Homestead steel strike
Catholic Church, and Knights of Labor, 51, 52
Central States Drivers Council, 140
Cheasty, John Cye, 139–140, **140**
Chicago, Ill., labor unrest in (*1886*), 55–58, **56–57**
Haymarket bombing in, 58–61, **59**
reaction to, 58–60
trial in, 60
Pullman strike, **title page**, 89, 95, 97
Army in, 96, **96–97**
Chicago *Inter Ocean*, quoted, 59
Child labor, 33, **33**, 35
Chinese Exclusion Act, 82
Chrysler Corporation, 118, 121
Cigarmakers International Union, 61, 72, 73, 75
organization of tenement workers, 69, 71
Cigarmaking industry, unionization of, 67–69 passim, 72, 73
and tenement workers, 69, 70, **70–71**, 71
CIO, see Committee for Industrial Organization; Congress of Industrial Organizations
Civil War, 40, 56
Clark, E. E., 79
Clayton Anti-Trust Act, 82–83
cartoon on, 83, **83**
Cleveland, Grover, President, 76, 83, 95
quoted, 97
use of Army in Pullman strike, 96, 97
Closed shop, 37, 128
Clothing Workers, Amalgamated, 115
Coal mining industry, unionization of, 76, 79
early strikes in, 76, 77, **77**
condition of workers in, 114, **114**
and captive mines, 114
advance of labor in, 125
World War II strikes in, 125
cartoon of disputes in postwar era, 126, **126**
Collective bargaining, principle of, 33, 82
Committee for Industrial Organization, formation and development of, 115, **115**, **116**, 117, 120, 122
Communism, 108–109, 130
in American unions, 7, 129–131, 134, 135, 145, 147
Congress of Industrial Organizations, 122–125 passim
Communists in, 129–131, 135
merger with A.F. of L., 125, 135, 136
see also Committee for Industrial Organization and AFL-CIO
Connecticut, labor legislation of, 34, 41
Constitution, U.S., 138, 139
Cotton textile industry, 24, **24**, 25–27, **27**, 29–30, 32, 33, 104
working conditions in, 7, 8, **9**, 29–30, 32, 35–36
Council of National Defense, 83

Curran, Joseph, 130, **130**
Curtis, Jennie, 94
Curtis, Dr. Josiah, quoted, 36

D

Daily Worker, 130
Darrow, Clarence, 101
Debs, Eugene Victor, quoted, 92
in cartoon, **88**, 89
early career of, 92, 94
described, 92
and Pullman strike, 92, 94, 95, 97
jailing of, 97–98
and Socialist Party, 98
as candidate for president, 98, **98**, 99, **99**
and IWW, 101
death of, 92, 98
Delaware, Lackawanna, and Western Railroad, 48
De Leon, Daniel, 99, 101
Denver Labor Enquirer, 52
Dickens, Charles, 29, 30
quoted, 25
Dubinsky, David, 115, 136, **136**

E

Eight-hour-day movement, 39, 41–42, 56, 61, 73, 75, 82, 83, 147
proclamation of, 43, **43**
effect of Haymarket affair on, 59
Eisenhower, Dwight D., President, 137
Engel, George, 60
execution of, **60**
Everest, Wesley, 108
quoted, 108

F

Factory Girls Association, 34
Factory system, 30, 33, 35
Federal Bureau of Investigation, 140
Federation of Organized Trades and Labor Unions of the United States and Canada, 56, 72–73
Fielden, Samuel, quoted, 58
and Haymarket bombing, 58, 60
Fifth Amendment, 138, 139
Firestone Tire Plant No. 1, Akron, Ohio, sit-down strike at, 117–118
Fischer, Adolph, 60
execution of, **60**
Flint Alliance, 120
Ford Motor Company, 118
automation of Cleveland engine works of, **146–147**, 147
Forty-hour week, 147
Frick, Henry Clay, 15–16, **20**, 109, 122
quoted, 17
and Homestead negotiations, 16–17
and Homestead strike, 18–21 passim

G

Gangsterism and crime, in unions, 7, 131, 134, 135, **144**, 145, 147
Garment cutters, unions of, 45–47 passim
Gary, Elbert H., 84–85
General Motors, 134
resistance to unions, 118, 120
sit-down strikes against, **118–119**, 119, 120–121, 122

Georgia, labor legislation of, 34
Gibbons, Cardinal, 52
Gladstone, William, 21
Goldman, Emma, 20, **20**
Gompers, Samuel, **66**, 67–87 passim, **87**, 98, 99, 100, 111, 112, 147
quoted, 68, 73, 75, 76, 80–81, 82, 87, 97
youth of, 67–69; ideology of, 68–69; personal difficulties of, 71; description of, 72; objectives of, 72, 74–76, 82
and cigarmakers' union, 69, 71–72, 73; organization and leadership of A.F. of L., 73, 74, 87; and defense of McNamara brothers, 81–82, **81**; and Commission on International Labor Legislation, 83; decline of, 83–84, 86, 87; death of, 87
relationships with: Terence Powderly, 73; Theodore Roosevelt, 75–76; James Van Cleave, 80–81; Woodrow Wilson, 83
Goodyear Tire and Rubber Company, 117
Gould, Jay, 53, 54, **54**
Grant, Ulysses S., President, 43
Great Britain, Industrial Revolution in, 25–26, 27
Great Northern Railway, 94
Greeley, Horace, **36**, 37
quoted, 35, 36
Green, William, 111, 112, 136, **136**
quoted, 113
cartoons of, 113, **113**, 116, **116**
as president of A.F. of L., 113, 115, 117, 125
death of, 135
Greenback-Labor Movement, 50

H

Hanna, Marcus, 76
Hanson, Harriet, quoted, 34
Harrison, Carter, 58
Hayes, John W., 65
Haymarket bombing, Chicago, 59, **59**, 60, 73
notice of meeting prior to, 56, **56–57**
effects of, 58–60, **60**, 61, 109
Haywood, "Big Bill," 98–99, **100**, 107
quoted, 99, 100, 109
and Steunenberg murder, 101
and IWW, 101, 103, 104, 108
convicted of conspiracy, 107–108
in Soviet Union, 109, **109**
Hill, James J., 94
Hill, Joe, 107
Hillman, Sidney, 115, **115**
Hirsch, David, 67, 68, 69
Hoffa, James Riddle, quoted, 139
background of, 138–139
elected president of Teamsters, 142–143
investigations of, 139–143 passim, **140**
arrest and convictions of, 140, 143
imprisonment of, 144, **144**
Homer, Winslow, painting by, **31**
Homestead, Pa., 10, **10–11**, 15
Homestead steel strike, 10, 11–15, **12**, **13**, **14**, **15**, 19–21, 75, 84, 122, 147
background of, 15–19
Pinkertons in, 12–15
consequences of, 21, 22·

casualties of, 13, 14, 15
Howard, Charles P., 115
Hutcheson, "Big Bill," 112, 113
  quoted, 111

I

Illinois, labor legislation of, 41
  and Haymarket bombing, 60–61
  coal mining in, 76, 112
Immigration, 35
  restriction of, 82
Industrial Revolution, 25–26
  second, 145
Industrial Workers of the World ("Wobblies"), 98, 101–109 passim
  posters of, 102, **102**
  cartoon of, 103, **103**
  rally of, 109, **109**
  formation of, 99–101
  membership of, 101, 103
  origin of nickname of, 103
  effect of World War I on, 107–109
International Ladies Garment Workers
  Union, 115
International Typographical Union, 72,
  115
Ireland, Archbishop, 76
Irish, immigration of, 35
Irish National Land League, 50
Iron industry, unionization of, 37–42
  passim
  poor working conditions in, 38, **38–39**
Iron Molders International Union, 40–42
Iron and Steel Workers, Amalgamated
  Association of, and Homestead strike,
  16–21 passim
Iron, Steel, and Tin Workers, Amal-
  gamated Association of, 84, 122
IWW, see Industrial Workers of the
  World

J

Jackson, Andrew, President, 26–27
Johnson, Andrew, President, 41, 43
Johnson, Malcolm, quoted, 133, 134
Johnston, Alvanley, 127
Journeyman Cordwainers, Federal So-
  ciety of, 32
Justice, U.S. Department of, 107
  "Hoffa unit," 143

K

Keller, K. T., 121
Kennedy, John F., President, 143
Kennedy, Robert F., Senator, quoted,
  137, 139
  and investigations of labor unions,
  136–143 passim, **141**
  investigation of Beck, 136–138
  investigation of Hoffa, 139–143
  as Attorney General, 143
Knights of Labor, Noble and Holy Order
  of, 45–65 passim
  poster of, **44**, 45
  emblem of, 47, **47**
  cartoon of, 62–63, **62–63**
  founding of, 45–47
  ritual and secrecy of, 46–47, **46**, 50–52
  District Assemblies of, 47
  General Assembly of (1878), 47–48

and Catholics, 51
growth of membership of, 54
effect of Haymarket affair on, 59–61
decline of, 64, 65, 73
Knudsen, William, 120

L

Labor, Secretary of, first, 82
Labor Day, New York parades, **cover**, 8,
  back endsheet
Labor legislation, 34–37 passim, 41–42,
  128
  see also specific acts
Labor Legislation, International Commission on, 83
Lawrence, Mass., textile strike at, 104–
  106, **105**, **106**
Lewis, John Llewellyn, 86, **110**, 111, 115,
  135
  quoted, 111, 114–115, 117, 121, 124,
  125, 129
  cartoons of, **113**, **116**, **123**, **126**
  early career of, 112
  famous eyebrows of, 121, 123
  characterized, 125
  and United Mine Workers, 112–114
  and industrial unionism, 112, 113–114,
  118
  and formation and growth of CIO, 115,
  118, 120–122, 129
  relationship with Franklin Roosevelt,
  122–124
  resignation from CIO, 124
  position on strikes during World War
  II, 125, 127
Lingg, Louis, 60
Little, Frank, 107
Little Bill (barge in Homestead strike),
  12, 13–14, 20
Lobby, labor, 37
Lockout, defined, 18
Locomotive Engineers, Brotherhood of,
  127
  certificate of membership, 92, **93**
Locomotive Firemen, Brotherhood of,
  92, 94
Loewe and Company, 80
Longshoremen's and Warehousemen's
  Union, International, Communism
  in, 130
  wildcat strike of, 132, **132–133**
  gangsterism in, 131, 133–134
Los Angeles Times, bombing of, **80–81**,
  81
Lowell, Francis Cabot, 26, 27
Lowell, Mass., cotton textile industry in,
  7, 25–35 passim, **30–31**, 89, 104
Lowell Female Labor Reform Associa-
  tion, 34
Lowell girls, working conditions of, 26–
  27, 29–30, 32–34, 147
Lowell Offering, quoted, 29–30
  title page of, 28, **28**
Lumbering industry, 103–104

M

McBride, John, 75
McClellan, John L., Senator, 136, 137,
  143
McCormick Harvester Company, 57–58

McKinley, William, President, 65, 75, 76
McNamara, John J. and James B., 81
Machinists and Blacksmiths, Interna-
  tional Union of, 48–49
Maine, labor legislation of, 34
Martin, Homer, 120
Martineau, Harriet, 27, 29
Marx, Karl, 42, 68
Mass production, 145
Massachusetts, labor legislation of, 35
Meany, George, 136, **136**
  quoted, 134, 143, 145
  and AFL-CIO, 135
  and automation, 145
Merrimack Manufacturing Company,
  26, 30
Merrimack River, 25, 26, **30–31**, 31, 104
Metal Workers, United, 99
Michigan, National Guard of, 120, 121
Missouri, labor legislation of, 41
Missouri Pacific Railroad, 54
Mitchell, John, 76, 79
Molly Maguires, 51, **51**
Moyer, Charles, 101
Murphy, Frank, Governor, 120–121
Murray, Philip, 115, **115**, 121, **121**, 124,
  125
  and organization of steel industry, 122
  and Communist issue, 130
  death of, 135

N

National Civic Federation, 76
National Industrial Recovery Act, 122–
  123
National Labor Relations Act, 123
National Labor Relations Board, 123
National Labor Union, 42, 72
National Maritime Union, 130
Neebe, Oscar, 60
New Deal, 122, 128
New England, cotton textile industry of,
  33, 35, 36
New Hampshire, labor legislation of,
  34–35
New York (state), labor legislation of, 41
  State Crime Commission of, 133
New York City, 12, 32, 47, 50, 68, 73,
  81, 87, 132, 136
  cigarmaking in, 69, **70–71**, 73
  Teamsters' power in, 140
  labor parades in, **cover**, 8, 149, **149**,
  back endsheet
New York Sun, quoted, 61
New York Times, 133
New-York Daily Tribune, 35, **36**

O

O'Donnell, Hugh, 11, 14, 15, 17, 19, **19**,
  21
Ohio, labor legislation of, 34
Olney, Richard, 95
Orchard, Harry, 101
Otis, Gen. Harrison Grey, 81

P

Parsons, Albert, 58, 60
  execution of, **60**
Paterson, N.J., iron foundry in, **38–39**,
  39

Pawtucket, R.I., cotton textile mills at, 27, **27**
Pennsylvania, National Guard of, 19, 20, 21, 79
 labor legislation of, 34
 coal mining industry of, 47, 50, 51, 76
 conditions of workers in, 114, **114**
 railroad strike in (*1877*), **48–49**, 50
Pettibone, George, 101
Philadelphia, Pa., 36, 38, 42, 79, 106
 shoemaking in, 32, **32**
 iron industry in, 38–40 *passim*
 tailors of, 45, 46
 formation of Knights of Labor in, 47
 steel strike in (*1919*), 84, **84**
Philadelphia and Reading Coal and Iron Company, 79
Pinkerton Detective Agency, 19, 147
 in Homestead strike, 12–15, **12**, **13**, **14**, **15**, 17
 casualties in, 13, 15
 and Molly Maguires, 51
Pittsburgh, Pa., 11, 12, 14, 15, 32, 72
 formation of Knights of Labor in, 47
 railroad violence in, 47, 49, **49**
 poor conditions in, 86
 and founding of A.F. of L., 87
Powderly, Terence V., **44**, 45
 quoted, 49, 50, 52, 56, 59–60, 64
 in cartoon, **65**
 background of, 48–49
 description and health of, 50–51, 53
 and Knights of Labor, 49–56 *passim*, 61, 64–65
 and Haymarket bombing, 59–61
 later career of, 65
 relationship with Gompers, 73
Pullman, George M., 89, 90–92, **90**, 95
Pullman, Ill., **90**, 92, 94
 described, 89–90
Pullman Palace Car Company, 91–92
 strike against, **title page**, 8, 94–95, **94–95**, 96, **96–97**, 97
 cartoon comment on, **88**, 89
Pullman sleeping cars, 89, 90, **90**, 95

Q

Quill, Mike, 130

R

Railroads, strikes against, 47, **48–49**, 49, 127
 brotherhoods of, characterized in cartoon, 62–63, **62–63**
 exploitation of miners, 76
Railway Conductors, Order of, 79
Railway Trainmen, Brotherhood of, 127
Raskin, A. H., quoted, 133
Reading, Pa., 48, 50
Reuther, Roy and Victor, 131, **131**
Reuther, Walter, 131, **131**, 145
 quoted, 131
 and Communists in unions, 130–131
 contributions of, 134–135
 and AFL-CIO, 135
Rhode Island, labor legislation of, 34
Riley, James Whitcomb, quoted, 92
Rockefeller, John D., Jr., 76
Roosevelt, Franklin D., President, 124, **124**

quoted, 123, 124
 and New Deal, 128
 relations with John L. Lewis, 122–124
Roosevelt, Theodore, President, 65, 75–76
 quoted, 76
 and coal strike (*1902*), 77, **77**, 79
Rubber industry, 117
Russia, *see* Soviet Union
Ryan, Joseph P., 133

S

Schnaubelt, Rudolph, 60
Schwab, Charles M., 21
Schwab, Michael, 60
Scranton, Pa., 48, 50, 76, 79
Senate, U.S., Select Committee on Improper Activities in the Labor or Management Field (Rackets Committee), 136–143 *passim*
Shenandoah, Pa., strike in (*1902*), 77, **77**
Sherman Anti-Trust Act, 80, 82, 95
Shoemaking, 32, **32**
Slater, Samuel, painting by, **27**
Snowden, Gen. George R., quoted, 19
Socialism, 68, 75, 98, 101
Socialist Party of America, 98
Socialist Trade and Labor Alliance, 99
Solidarity, masthead of, 102, **102**
Soviet Union, Communism in, 103, 108–109, 129, 131
 and Cold War, 129
Spies, August, 57–58
 quoted, 57, 60
 arrest and execution of, 60, **60**
Steel industry, working conditions in, 16, **16**, 17, 21, **22–23**, 23, 84–85, 86
 unionization of, 15, 16, 85, 121, 122, 123
 strike against (*1919*), 85, **85**, 86
 and "captive coal mines," 114–115
Steel Workers' Organizing Committee, 122
Stephens, Uriah, **44**, 54
 and Knights of Labor, 45–46, 50
Steunenberg, Frank, Governor, murder of, 101
Strasser, Adolph, and Cigarmakers' International Union, 69, 71–72, 73
 and A.F. of L., 73
Strikes, jurisdictional, 129
Supreme Court, U.S., 80, 81, 122–123, 143
Sylvis, William H., 37–42 *passim*, **41**, 56, 72, 147
 quoted, 38, 39, 41, 42

T

Taft, Robert A., Senator, 128, **128**
Taft-Hartley Act, 128–129, 135
 cartoon on, 126, **126**
Talmadge, A. A., 53
Taylor, Myron C., 122
Teamsters, International Brotherhood of, growth of, 139–140
 investigations of officers of, 136–138, 142
 loyalty of, to Hoffa, 144, **144**
 alliance with UAW, 146
Ten-hour day, 34–35, 36

Texas Pacific Railroad, 55
Textile industry, *see* Cotton textile industry
Tompkins Square, New York City, melee in, 68, 69, **69**, 73
Transport Workers Union, 130
Troy, N.Y., 40
Truman, Harry S., President, quoted, 127
 in cartoon, 126, **126**
 and railroad strike (*1946*), 127
 and labor legislation, 128

U

Union Pacific Railroad, 52–53
Union Square, New York City, rally in, 109, **109**, **back endsheet**
United Automobile Workers, organization and growth of, 118, 120, 121, 125, 130, 134
 sit-down strike of, **118–119**, 119
 alliance with Teamsters, 145–146
United Electrical, Radio and Machine Workers Union, 129, 131
United Hatters Union, 80
United Mine Workers, 75, 82, 86, 100, 117, 124–125, 127, 135
 certificate of membership, 78, **78**
 growth and development of, 76, 79, 111, 112, 114–115
United Nations, International Labor Organization of, 137
U.S. Steel Corporation, 22, 122
 strike against (*1919*), 84–85, **84**
United Steelworkers of America, 122

V

Van Buren, Martin, President, 34
Van Cleave, James, 80–81

W

Wabash Railroad, 55
Wagner Act, *see* National Labor Relations Act
Waltham, Mass., 26, 30, 32
Washington, D.C., 32, 37, 115
 as A.F. of L. headquarters, 75, 83, 87
Western Federation of Miners, 99, 100–101
Whitney, A. F., 127
Whittier, John Greenleaf, quoted, 7
Williams, Edward B., 138, **138**
Willkie, Wendell, 124
Wilson, William B., 82
Wilson, Woodrow, President, 82, 83
 quoted, 82
 campaign button of, 82, **82**
Wisconsin, labor legislation of, 41
Wise, Rabbi Stephen, 85
Wobblies, *see* Industrial Workers of the World
Women, in cotton textile industry, 8, 9, 33–35
 see also Lowell girls
Women's rights movement, 42
Woodstock, Ill., McHenry County Jail in, 97
World War I, 83, 98, 104, 107, 108, 145
World War II, 129, 131, 145
 labor during, 125, 127
 unrest following, 127–128

153